Exploring the Psychosocial and Psycho-spiritual Dynamics of Singleness among African American Christian Women in Midlife

Exploring the Psychosocial and Psycho-spiritual Dynamics of Singleness among African American Christian Women in Midlife

CHRISTINA HICKS

WIPF & STOCK · Eugene, Oregon

EXPLORING THE PSYCHOSOCIAL AND PSYCHO-SPIRITUAL DYNAMICS
OF SINGLENESS AMONG AFRICAN AMERICAN CHRISTIAN WOMEN IN
MIDLIFE

Wipf & Stock
An Imprint of Wipf and Stock Publishers
199 W. 8th Ave., Suite 3
Eugene, OR 97401

www.wipfandstock.com

PAPERBACK ISBN: 971-5326-1951-9
HARDCOVER ISBN: 978-1-4982-4583-8
EBOOK ISBN: 978-1-4982-4582-1

Manufactured in the U.S.A.   JULY 31, 2017

Contents

CONTENTS

Introduction

The Birthing Process

The impetus for this research was birthed out of many conversations with African American women, both single and married alike. Several years ago, I had the pleasure of leading a women's ministry group in my church. The goal of this ministry was to build and foster relations with the women of my church and to tackle some of the issues that were prevalent for African American women. This group consisted of a range of young adult women and older midlife women. Some were married and some single; others were single mothers, divorced and widowed. After meeting for some time, I began to notice that all of our conversations, no matter what topic we were discussing, or no matter what readings we were examining, almost always led to questions about sex, singleness, loneliness, dating and marriage. "Is there a proper way to live a single life?" "What does God require?" "Is sex off limits to Christian single women?" "I'm lonely and I don't know what to do?" These are some of the questions that surfaced during "the talk." Several of the married women had similar questions about their sexuality and loneliness within their own marriages. I also had similar questions about my own singleness. When I tried having serious discussions with my peers, ordained female ministers like myself, I was told quite caustically, "You need to stand in your authority!" I've learned over the course of years that the church space is not always a safe place to discuss my sacred issues. At the time, I was a much younger single African American woman, now I am a much older midlife single African American woman. With this understanding, I believe that singleness from the perspective of twenty- and thirty-year-old women is much different than the perspective of forty- and fifty-year-old women. As such, this research explores the experiences of singleness from a midlife perspective. Several years later, I continue with these discussions on singleness with midlife women who question their purpose amidst singleness, dating, growing older, childlessness and spirituality. These discussions constitute the birthing process of many explorations into singleness that have been gained over the years from my own experiences and from the experiences of numerous single African American women that I've had the pleasure of having these important and heartfelt conversations into what it means to be single, African American, and a woman.

THE PRINCIPAL QUESTION AND PROBLEM

The principal question addressed in this research is: *How does singleness impact the lives of African American Christian women in midlife?* There have been many discussions in the African American community and the Black church about the disproportionate number of African American men to the number of single African American women.

> According to "Single, Black, Female—and Plenty of Company" forty-two percent of U.S. black women have never been married, double the number of white women who have never tied the knot. . . . There are 1.8 million more black women than black men. If every black man in America married a black woman today, one out of every 12 lack women still wouldn't make it down the aisle if they hope to marry a black man.[1]

The issue is that many African American women, Christian and non-Christian, are frustrated in their search for eligible African American men to date and/or marry. Although more people are choosing to remain single in the twenty-first century, both the culture and the church milieus dictate marriage as the idealized state for most. Many single African American women are concerned about the shortage of "good African American men." While many factors contribute to the issue of singleness, certain ones are dominant in the African American community. "Racism, high mortality and incarceration rates, and economic disadvantage in obtaining skills necessary for upward mobility have decreased the pool of marriageable men."[2] Another factor that contributes to the problem of "singleness" is that most

---

1. Davis and Karar, "Single, Black, Female," lines 9–14.
2. Berliner et al., "Single Adults and the Life Cycle," 165.

single middle-class educated African American women feel less inclined to marry below their standards. For some, only men with an equivalent or higher educational and socioeconomic status are acceptable. As a result, a large number of African American women are single because they choose not to marry or even date men below their standards.

In religious circles, most societies have adopted some suitable means of being single. "Singleness during adolescence and early adulthood, and following the death of a spouse has been acceptable in most societies."[3] However, few provisions are made for singleness outside of these parameters. "Except for those who entered religious orders, being single was not ideally the desired state for most individuals."[4] Because the institution of marriage is considered the ideal state, many single people use this to assess whether or not something is deficient or even wrong in their lives.[5] Some find themselves in a reactive position to what the culture dictates as normal.[6] If marriage is not achieved by certain parameters, it has a "direct impact on their sense of place within the culture, their position within the family structure, and their evaluation of self."[7]

THE EXPLORATION PROCESS

According to Mary Lynn Dell in "Will My Time Ever Come? On Being Single," "The implications of being a single woman vary tremendously according to race, ethnicity, religion, socioeconomic status, educational level, and geographic location."[8] Single women are all ages and come from all walks of life. They are bisexual, heterosexual or homosexual.[9] They are divorced, widowed, or single parents. Not all women want to marry; many single women choose to be single. For the purposes of this research, I engaged three heterosexual single African American Christian women who have never been married, have no children and are between the ages of forty and fifty-five to whom I have given the following names: "Diane," "Angie," and "Tracy."

3. Staples, "Black Singles in America," 40.

4. Ibid.

5. Schwartzberg et al., *Single in a Married World*, 4.

6. Ibid.

7. Ibid.

8. Dell, "Will My Time Ever Come?," 312.

9. Ibid.

Diane: is a 43-year-old single, middle-class African American woman who is the younger of two sisters. Diane works as a paralegal and has an associate's degree in marketing and a bachelors of theology. Her religious affiliation is Christian and she attends a nondenominational and nontraditional Black church. Being a Christian means to be a "follower of the way and to love God and love others." She describes her life while growing up as "unbalanced," "a mess," "turmoil," and "fighting," as her mom tried to keep it all together in an estranged marriage.

Angie: is a 48-year-old single, middle-class African American woman who is the oldest of five siblings—she is the oldest of two from her parent's marriage and the oldest of three from her father's relationship after her parents divorced. Angie works as an assistant director in research and as a senior pastor of a traditional church. She earned a bachelors degree in journalism and religious studies and a Master of Divinity. Her parents are both educators and throughout her life stressed the importance of education. Angie's parents divorced when she was eleven years old and she recalls the difficulties in her parents' marriage. Despite this, her home environment was very "loving." Angie understands that being a Christian means to "follow Jesus Christ." However it also means that God "reveals" God's self in a multiplicity of ways.

Tracy: is a 53-year-old single, middle-lass African American woman who is a project consultant and has some formal college education and is pursuing a bachelors degree in social work, ministry and context. She is the oldest of two from her parents' marriage and is the fourth child of her father's, including a previous marriage. Tracy viewed her parent's marriage as "healthy" and they were attentive and active in her life. Her faith tradition is nontraditional and she believes that being a Christian means confessing Jesus Christ as Lord and Savior.

Throughout this discourse I refer to them as single African American Christian women (SAACW) in midlife. They serve as the informants of this research and it is their narratives and voices that guide many of the findings reported in the chapters. They offer significant insights into singleness from many perspectives in midlife. My reasons for this selection stem from the existential questions voiced by them and what it means to be human/single living without husbands, children and traditional families. I have chosen the case study method of research as a means of discovering insights from "Diane," "Angie," and "Tracy." The exploration process begins with the sociocultural phenomenon of singleness and African American women. How this sociocultural phenomenon impacts SAACW and their understanding of the self is fundamental to this research. Other research questions that were of importance include:

1. What are the sociocultural, emotional, familial, sexual-spiritual, psychological, ethical and theological narratives of SAACW in midlife?

2. What are the experiences, questions, myths, and beliefs that are derived from singleness?

3. How might this research bring awareness to SAACW in midlife, religious communities and the Black church?

THE BLACK CHURCH

This exploration of singleness is situated socially in the Black church. As many of the members of the Black church are female, it is important to discuss how religion impacts and frames this discourse. SAACW have many embedded beliefs about singleness as told from their church leadership and supported by many moralistic precepts outlined in the Bible. Sexuality and spirituality present many paradoxical challenges to SAACW intensified by the Black church's understanding of sexuality and spirituality. Kelly Brown Douglas, in *Sexuality and the Black Church*, posits that "the manner in which Black women are treated in many Black churches reflects Western Christian tradition's notion of women as evil and its notions of Black women as Jezebels and seducers of men."[10] Several questions come to mind in relation to sexuality. What are SAACW's attitudes toward their own sexuality? Should SAACW be able to express themselves fully as sexual beings without feeling any guilt and shame or without being labeled as Jezebels and seducers of men? Singleness in the Black church is as much a relationship problem as it is a sexual problem. The deviancy of singleness is explored and interpreted within the confines of the narratives, experiences and lived realities of SAACW. Furthermore, the Black church is a strong familial and extended familial institution and how this impacts

10. Brown-Douglas, *Sexuality and the Black Church*, 83.

SAACW and their existential questions about love, relationship and family is endemic to this discourse.

RESEARCH METHODOLOGY

The research methodology used for this study is qualitative research using the narratives of three SAACW in midlife. This research design allows an in-depth and interpretive framework for the experiences of African American women and it is best suited for highlighting cultural distinctions. Combined with narrative approaches, it is instrumental in informing various dynamics that shape race and gender interactions. One of the challenges of empirical research is that it has often characterized African American women negatively, failing to make meaningful conceptual distinctions across race and gender.[11] However, a Black feminist and womanist analysis emphasizes the absolute necessity of Black women to be empowered to speak from and about their own experiential location.[12] I have chosen a liberating intercultural praxis as a pastoral theological methodology. Emmanuel Y. Lartey, in *Pastoral Theology in an Intercultural World*, emphasizes the social and cultural realities that are foundational to this method. African American women's experiences are both socially and culturally constructed through individual and collective contexts. Lartey's *Liberating Intercultural Praxis* is a multilayered contextual approach that takes into consideration gender, race, class, culture, faith, and ethics as a means of engagement.[13] By integrating an intercultural praxis with womanist themes this study becomes a liberating work that illumines the experiences of SAACW that are central to this research. The first step in the *Liberating Intercultural Praxis* is the constructed reality and the contextual experience that is situated socially and culturally. The second step is the contextual analysis that examines closely those social and cultural realties and experiences. The third step is the theological analysis and faith questions that are formulated in those lived experiences and realities. The fourth step includes the theological implications that are explored over and against many faith questions and existential concerns. The fifth step integrates the contextual experiences, constructed realities, contextual analysis and theological analysis to include an appropriate theological response and pastoral practice.

11. Few et al., "Sister-to-Sister Talk," 207.

12. Ibid.

13. Lartey, *Pastoral Theology*, 89.

Similarly, social constructivism and critical race theory are two interpretive and worldview lenses that guide this research. In *social constructivism* "individuals seek understanding in the world in which they live and work."[14] Individuals develop meanings from these experiences and interpret them from various social locations. In this case, social constructivism is a theoretical tool that explores the sociocultural norms that are endemic to SAACW and explores the meanings that they associate with these norms. *Critical Race Theory* (CRT) is an empowerment tool that takes into consideration an analysis of race, class and gender as a mode of social change. It concentrates on the narratives and counter-narratives from the vantage point of the oppressed and challenges the dominant culture's accepted truths. SAACW hold a unique place in American culture and society, and their stories challenge many of the "myths" of singleness that infiltrate the Black church and society. Alongside these interpretive and worldview lenses are narrative approaches that provide a rich and exploratory base for examining the voices, stories, myths and beliefs of SAACW. From the narratives of SAACW, I employ eight multifaceted lenses that illuminate this experience: sociocultural, emotional, familial, sexual-spiritual, theological, psychological, ethical and pastoral. In pursuit of this, I integrate what has been discussed in religious contexts, sociocultural contexts, popular culture and social media and put them in conversation with the multifaceted experiences of the SAACW examined in the chapters.

OUTLINE OF CHAPTERS

Chapter 1 begins with several conversations about the shortage of *good* African American men and the problem with single African American women that are discussed in popular culture. This dialogue explores the *wrongness* that is often associated with older single women who have been single for prolonged periods of time. Chapter 2 is the socio-contextual analysis of this research whereby singleness is examined from various individual, communal and religious contexts. A thematic narrative analysis provides a more in-depth dialogue about the experiences of SAACW in contemporary American culture.

As such, chapter 3 examines the midlife journey as explored by Natalie Schwartzberg, Kathy Berliner and Demaris Jacob in *Single in a Married World: A Life Cycle Framework for Working with the Unmarried Adult*. These

14. Creswell, *Qualitative Inquiry*, 24.

authors place a therapeutic emphasis on singleness from the perspective of the midlife cycle and the emotional issues that develop as a result of being unmarried and without children. Chapter 4 takes a look at the *ideal* family concept that is promoted in the society and the Black church. Several idyllic and mythical perceptions of marriage and family are challenged.

Chapter 5 examines sexuality and spirituality from womanist perspectives and Christian lenses. This chapter considers many of the religious myths and stereotypes that inform sexual behavior and how this is interpreted by SAACW. Next, a theological metaphor of singleness that speaks to the theological questions and specific needs of SAACW is examined in chapter 6. How SAACW understand their humanity in the midst of church and society is explored.

As a psychological framework, the Stone Center and relational-cultural theory reframes women's relationships as they are formulated in the dominant culture. In chapter 7, I explore relational-cultural theory in the Black church as a practical resource for developing a healthiness of the self for SAACW. And finally, chapter 8 explores pastoral theological strategies for church ministry to SAACW along with approaches to self-care.

Chapter 1

"What's Wrong with You and Why Aren't You Married?"

SAACW IN MIDLIFE: THE BLACK CHURCH AND SOCIETY

Two years ago, I attended a theological conference where I met several African American women professors, scholars, ministers, clinical practitioners and doctoral candidates in the field of pastoral theology and counseling. An invitation was extended by an African American female professor to all of the African American women in attendance to meet later that evening for an impromptu gathering. As we gathered that evening and made our introductions, a twenty-two-year-old woman, who turned out to be the youngest woman in the room, introduced herself and explained that this conference was recommended by a friend in ministry. As she continued with her introduction she said, "I just want to know one thing, why it is that the White women attending this conference are here with their husbands but none of the Black women are here with their husbands?" "Why are the Black women here by themselves?" "Why are Black women always by themselves?" You could hear a pin drop; there was a dead silence in the room. She went on further to say, "When I go back home all the young Black girls in my church will want to know about the women I've met and their families, husbands or boyfriends. One professor explained that she was an African American lesbian and that the culture and society would not allow her to marry (this was before the Supreme Court ruling on same-sex marriage). Another professor said, "Well, you know we are all talented and gifted Black women," but that didn't explain why we were a group of talented, gifted and *single* Black women. The rest of us sat in stunned silence and disbelief. No one else mentioned their marital status (I wasn't married) when she asked the question, so I assumed that we were all single African American women (at least the women in this gathering) in the room. Everyone seemed uncomfortable with the question because we stared off in space and the energy definitely shifted in the room. The question caught us off guard. We moved on to other conversation, but no one said anything about the topic except the two female professors. Afterward, some of us had a conversation with the young woman in the corner to explain why we were single, because at least for me the question left a funny taste in my mouth, metaphorically speaking. Why did I and others feel a need to explain our marital status to someone we just met? Why did it make us uncomfortable? Why did this question coming from a young twenty-something woman bother me, a single midlife Christian woman?

I believe that the question asked by the young woman and other conversations about single African American women are concerned with the question: *"What's wrong with you and why aren't you married?"* Although there are single women of all ethnicities, single African American women are scrutinized more often than any other group for their marital status and the lack of eligible men that are accessible to marry single African American women. The cultural perception is that African American women are the least likely to marry out of all ethnicities and that 70 percent of African American women will remain single for the rest of their lives.[1] Several reasons are cited for the groups of African American women who are unmarried in the following social communications.

According to an April 2015 Brookings Institution study on social mobility, "There is a growing trend in the United States toward assortative mating—a clunky phase that refers to people's tendency to choose spouses with similar educational attainment."[2] Educational compatibility is crucial in assortative mating because the economic boost between two educated partners is significant. African American families are directly impacted by the economic disparity that exists between the disproportionate numbers of educated African American men that are accessible to the number of educated African American women.[3]

1. James, "Why Most Black Women," line 1.

2. Rodrigue and Reeves, "Single Black Female," line 1.

3. The American Community Survey also referenced in the Brookings Institution

In addition to the 2015 Brookings Institution study, Ralph Richard Banks, in *Is Marriage for White People: How the African American Marriage Decline Affects Everyone* (2011), explores the evolving relationship market for Black women and the disproportionate number of Black men for them to marry. Banks gives three major contributors to the man shortage:

> First, Black men's incarceration constricts the market for poor and working-class Black women, second, interracial marriage depletes the pool of men for middle-class, college-educated Black women, and third, the economic prospects for many men have worsened while those for women have improved.[4]

As well, in "Why Educated, Single, Black Women Struggle to Marry," Black women give their perspective on marriage and whether or not this is a possibility for the future. Many believe that there is not a "large enough pool of their equals to choose a husband."[5] While Black men are more likely to date and marry outside of their race, Black women are 2.5 times less likely to date or marry outside of their race than their male counterparts.[6] Other factors in this discussion include an increasing number of available men who are waiting to marry later in life. This is a source of frustration for single twenty- to thirty-year-old African American females who are ready to marry.[7] Paradoxically, this places older single African American females in a precarious situation. What we have is large pools of older never-been-married African American females who remain unmarried because of the reasons stated above and other personal and religious factors.

As a final point, many question and blame the Black church for so many single and lonely African American women. In April 2010, CNN explored this issue in "Does the Black Church Keep Black Women Single?" This article begins with a strong assertion by Deborrah Cooper, a writer for the San Francisco *Examiner* and the blog SurvivingDating.com, in which claims were made about mainline protestant Black churches and their role

---

Study, examined Black-White marriage rates by education and race: Young White women—aged between 25 and 35—are the most likely to have a BA (37%), followed by White men (29%), Black women (23%), and Black men (16%). This analysis focused on a 25- to 35-year-old age cohort because these are the years during which most women, particularly college graduates, enter into their first marriage.

4. Banks, *Marriage*, 29.

5. Ellie, "Educated, Single Black Women," line 6.

6. Ibid., line 7.

7. Ibid., line 10.

in "blinding Black women in their search for love."[8] This, Cooper asserts, is due to the rhetoric of conventional Black church ideologies that perpetuate submissive roles of women. These ideologies are conveyed mostly by Black male leaders who "encourage women to be patient instead of getting up and going after what they want, which may mean going to another church or leaving the church to go where the boys go: tailgates, bars and clubs."[9] With this understanding, Cooper suggests that Black women should consider other social arenas to meet men other than the church. Cooper states:

> Black women need to open their eyes. You want to know the rea-
> son why the Black man isn't in church? Because he left church to
> go to the Sunday football game. . . . Going to these sites is discour-
> aged in the Black church because these places are seen as places
> where "sin dwells." But if women are compassionate, as the Bible
> preaches they should be, then they need to be more open about
> the men they choose to date and where they might meet them.[10]

Thus, Cooper's point of contention is that Black women limit themselves from meeting potential suitors because of the pedagogy of the Black church. In rebuttal to Cooper's argument, Renita J. Weems, a notable bibli-cal scholar and author of women's spirituality, cautions against Cooper's premise because it reinforces one message: "It's the Black woman's fault."[11]

The collective consensus is that single African American women's failure to marry is a reflection of their womanhood and a result of being born Black and female. Many images are widely circulated in contempo-rary culture and they give distinct impressions about the plight of single African American women. The public scrutiny blames educational dispar-ity between African American men and women, high incarceration rates, interracial marriage and economic challenges for African American men along with embedded cultural beliefs and damaging religious ideology for African American women. For SAACW, these statements along with other specific images are depicted in religious, familial and communal settings. Therefore, this chapter examines the diverse cultural images of SAACW that are reinforced in the Black church and society.

8. Membis, "Does the Black Church," line 12.

9. Ibid., lines 20, 53.

10. Ibid., lines 54–58.

11. Ibid., line 42.

CULTURAL IMAGES OF SAACW IN MIDLIFE

"You Must Be a Lesbian"

With the predominance of cultural images and stereotypes that are reinforced in the church and society, SAACW face many obstacles. For example, if they have not subscribed to the expected roles of wife or mother, if they have chosen a different path other than marriage or if marriage opportunities have not presented themselves in the expected young adulthood time frame, then this behavior is viewed suspiciously by those in the Black church and society. The suspicion is even greater for older single women who have been single for a prolonged period of time. Although the traditional roles of women have changed and evolved over the years, there is a lingering suspicion that looms over the lives of African American women who are older, midlife, single and unmarried.

A cultural distortion that is controversial in the way that it depicts SAACW is the image of *lesbian*. In this discourse, it is not my intention to suggest that there is anything wrong with women who are lesbian. The wrongness as I perceive it has to do with the harmful influence of a society that uses labels, titles and misrepresentations against women (and men) to support their intolerance against difference and preference. Thus, lesbian is defined as "women who are primarily attracted emotionally, physically, spiritually, and sexually to other women."[12] The implication of this term suggests that SAACW have hidden secretive lives and sexual relations with other women and this is the sole reason they are single and unmarried. The potential apprehension that is voiced by family, friends, and church members along with the stigma that the term lesbian carries in the culture, church and society presents several challenges.[13]

Remarks referring to their perceived lesbian status are meant to cast suspicion and doubt upon their sexuality and sexual orientation. The underlying bias is that their presumed lesbian status needs *straightening out*. In other words, sexual contact with men will make them less suspicious in the eyes of those who question their sexual orientation. Terms such as *straight* and *crooked* have been used to represent one's sexual status. Heterosexuals are categorized as straight and non-heterosexuals are categorized as crooked. The understanding here is that these labels impose a sexual stigma

12. Marshall, "Sexual Identity," 143.
13. Ibid.

on heterosexual SAACW, not to mention that they are offensive to those in the Lesbian, Gay, Bisexual and Transgendered (LGBT) community.

Furthermore, SAACW who are labeled as lesbian are portrayed as women who are *unattractive, unwomanly* and have *difficulty in holding a man's attention*. For African American women there is the stigma surrounding their self image and the acceptance associated with their skin color, hair texture, body images and facial features.[14] Historically, these assertions have been distorted by European Americans and have a lasting impact on the self-esteem of African American women. Nonetheless, these same distortions about skin color, hair texture, body image and facial features that have been historically perpetuated by European Americans have been internalized in the mind-sets and behaviors of African American people. How skin color, hair texture, body image and facial features intersect with other perceived notions of physical attraction is explored below.

When the physical appearance of SAACW is perceived as masculine, and in particular if the hair is "natural," "short razor haircut," or "shaved head" and if the clothing is perceived as *manly* or body type is *athletic* then they are labeled as *dykes, bull dyke* or *butch*, "a derogatory label to describe masculine or butch lesbians."[15] "This stereotype includes the belief that bull dykes are aggressive, objectively unattractive, and man-hating."[16] The idea is that heterosexual SAACW may fear that African American men will find them unattractive with natural hair or they may feel that their behavior is seen as too aggressive, assertive or masculine.

This type of dissension is also carried over into their friendships and girlfriend networks. Many SAACW feel that they have to censor their language about their long-term close female friends for fear of being labeled a lesbian. *My girlfriend*, a term used in general conversations with friends, family and church members, takes on a new meaning and is often misconstrued to mean a secret lesbian relationship and attraction. For many single women across all racial lines, girl-friends or sister-friends provide tremendous support and sometimes familial relationships with unmarried women. For this reason, *girlfriends* are not meant to carry a sexual overtone.

The image of lesbian also presents other challenges and biases in the form of discrimination. In the Western culture there is discrimination in

14. Jackson, "New Multiculturalism," 9.
15. Ward, "Bull Dyke," 492.
16. Ibid.

support of those who are in opposite sex relationships.[17] It is important to note "the rights and unearned advantages bestowed by heterosexual or straight privilege in society."[18] However, the problem lies in a culturally insensitive society where individuals are ridiculed according to race, ethnicity, gender, sex-orientation, age, religion, disability, culture, socioeconomic status and in this discourse singleness. The essence of this understanding is that heterosexual SAACW and those who are discriminated against in this society cannot live authentically as those created and affirmed in the image of God.

"The Sinister Reason" (Eve)

In contrast, the image of Eve has a profound impact on SAACW in midlife. The story of Eve's deception in the creation story, Gen 2–3, has been widely associated with women and their perceived dysfunction in the church and society. Because Eve has been labeled as *evil, deceitful, sinful, seductive, harlot*, and *whore*, all women have inherited these negative attributes. Eve is chastised for leading her husband into sin, Eve represents everything that is wrong in all women; and women are cursed by the sin and sexuality of Eve.[19] "Even Paul in 1 Timothy blames Eve (and, hence her descendants) for her alleged susceptibility of deceit: It was not Adam who[m] [the serpent] deceived; it was the woman who, yielding to deception, fell into sin (1 Tim 2:14; cf. Gen 3)."[20]

Feminist and womanist scholarship challenges patriarchal interpretations that threaten "women's spirits, bodies, agency and power both in Scripture texts and in reception of those texts."[21] The reading and reception of Gen 2–3 and 1 Tim 2:14 are generalizations and interpretations of biblical texts that require far more careful and contextual scrutiny. Because of Eve's alleged deceit, women are often pitted against one another because trust is an issue with women who are perceived as deceitful. This distrust also plays out in relationships between married and single women. The dichotomy that exists is an "us against them, a single versus married" mental-

17. On June 26, 2015, the Supreme Court legalized same sex marriage across the United States.

18. Iyer, "Heterosexual Privilege," 418.

19. Bellis, *Helpmates, Harlots, and Heroes*, 38.

20. Harris, *New Testament*, 342.

21. Sharp, *Wrestling with the Word*, 120.

ity. Married women are allegedly suspicious or threatened by single women because they fear that they will attempt to seduce their husbands. Single women are allegedly envious of married women because married women have something that they don't have. Alice Ogden Bellis, in *Helpmates, Harlots, and Heroes: Women's Stories in the Hebrew Bible*, states that the story of "Eve is interpreted and shaped in ways that have a lasting influence on Western understandings of women's status, roles and places an emphasis on women's sin and inferiority."[22] The "sinister reason" is based on interpretations that are reiterated and embedded within the psyches of women and men in the life of the Black church and society. It also implies that there is some ominous sinful reason that is lurking beneath the surface that keeps SAACW single and it calls into question their sexual and moral character.

"What's Wrong with You and Why Aren't You Married?"

Historically, women in the Black church and society were raised to believe that their primary role was to get married and have children. Although traditional settings have changed in some respects, there is the lingering stigma for women who seek alternative lives to marriage and motherhood. The stigma suggests that something is wrong with women who are single or choose to remain single for a myriad of reasons. Many social and religious institutions are still relegated to a traditional family environment and usually don't consider singleness as a normative way of life. In the Black church environment the life and spirituality of the community is very much organized around marriage and family. Single people are often encouraged to marry and start families of their own. People don't quite know what to say and do for midlife women who have surpassed the median age for marriage and having children.

"Diane," a participant in this study was asked, *"What's wrong with you and why aren't you married?"* The implication of this question is that something is wrong with women who have been unsuccessful in finding a partner or who have no interest and desire to partner. The judgment is that there is some innate pathology in African American women who find themselves man-less, child-less or seeking companionship. Much like the larger single population is comprised of many diverse people who are unmarried for various reasons, SAACW are not pathological, abnormal or suffering from mental challenges because they are single.[23] In a culture

22. Ibid., 39.
23. Ibid., 314.

that discriminates against African American women because of their race, gender, class and marital status, these labels imply that they do not posses values and virtues worthy of marriage.

"What's wrong with you and why aren't you married?" Some implications are that African American women are *emotionally bereft, too difficult to get along with, angry, argumentative, demanding* or *they have too many problems.* All too often women and especially African American women are deemed as pathological in environments they hold as sacred. Singleness in and of itself is not a sufficient reason in environments where marriage is seen as the club that everyone belongs to.

"How Old Are You?"

Another cultural image that accounts for certain biases and discrimination against older unmarried women and which has a definite impact on the image of SAACW is the stereotype of *old maid* and *spinster*. Historically, "single women were viewed as so evil and subversive that they faced not only stigma but overt violence."[24] "During the 1600s and 1700s in New England, single women (and especially those over the age of forty) were particularly vulnerable to being convicted of witchcraft or even put to death."[25] Several definitions of the term *spinster* are as follows:

> The terms *bachelor* and *spinster* refer to the civic status of never being married, though they have more commonly been used to describe those remaining unmarried beyond conventional marriage age. . . . The term *spinster*, literally "one who spins," relates to the expected task of the unmarried woman in the Anglo-Saxon households, that of spinning yarn. The word came to signify unmarried women in legal documents from the 17th century. . . . Stereotypes attached to bachelorhood and spinsterhood vary in relation to particular historical and cultural contexts. The many negative synonyms used historically for spinsters, such as "odd," "redundant," and "old maid," are indicative of the different significance marriage has held for women and men. . . . Historically, the spinster was depicted as a pitiable victim of circumstance, "on the shelf" due to a shortage of men following war or having to care for parents. The modern spinster is more often depicted as pursuing

24. Anderson and Stewart, *Flying Solo*, 51.
25. Ibid.

a career at the expense of marriage and motherhood. Both, however, are represented as ultimately unfulfilled.[26]

The historical images of single women in the 1600s and 1700s give an
unsettling account of single women forced to live on the periphery of society. While singleness is more of an acceptable option today, several assumptions, attitudes and beliefs still prevail. One assumption is that SAACW are
perceived as spinsters who are able to give more of their time, energy and
resources to their churches and jobs because they don't have families. As
described above, the role of the caregiver is the default position of the spinster woman. Another assumption is that an older single spinster woman is
unfulfilled and in some respects is a failure in life.

Moreover, the impact of sexism and ageism are even more prominent
in a youth-driven society. The value of growing old is not readily accepted by
those in mainstream society. An "old maid" in Western culture is one who
is past her prime, over the hill in age and has never married. The mental
image of an old maid is one who is stereotypically a loser, unattractive and
depressed. Furthermore, an old maid is "on the shelf due to a shortage of men
following war."[27] The African American male shortage falsely categorizes
SAACW as older, lonely, desperate, sexually frustrated "women on the shelf."
Modern day *cougars* are older women who financially support younger men
in exchange for companionship, sexual or otherwise. The perception is that
they are willing to accept any proposal because there is "slim pickings," an old
adage that means there are few options available to them. Since their options
are so limited, they are willing to fall prey as the *side-piece*, which equates to
the other woman on the side who is not the wife or the main girlfriend. The
misconception is that SAACW are willing to go to any lengths to secure the
attention of a man in the hopes of obtaining a husband.

Another image that contrasts with the spinster and old maid stereotype is that of "Miss Independent" as described by Electra S. Gilchrist
in "Neither an 'Old Maid' nor a 'Miss Independent': Deflating the Negative Perceptions of Single African American Women Professors."[28] The
"modern spinster is one depicted as pursuing her career at the expense
of marriage and motherhood."[29] Professional African American women
are labeled as modern spinsters who are "too independent when they can

26. Simpson, "Bachelors and Spinsters," 51.
27. Ibid.
28. Gilchrist, "Neither an 'Old Maid,'" 177.
29. Ibid.

provide for themselves financially without the help of male providers."[30] Those who fit in this category are able to achieve the niceties of life without the confines of marriage. However the negative aspect of this achievement is that they are perceived as women who are uninterested in marriage and therefore are to blame for undermining the institution of marriage. Furthermore, single professional women and especially African American women who are financially independent are seen as a threat to the men that they potentially want to date or even marry. Educated, financially savvy African American women are often identified as dominating women who emasculate African American men. Gilchrist asserts that the "independent and self sufficient demeanors of professional African American women often further stereotype them as opinionated, unwilling to listen, and unable to submit."[31] Another caveat is that financial independence equates to strength, and for African American women strength is viewed as a destructive force interpersonally. Hence, fiercely independent women are not well received by the men they partner with because independence is perceived as a source of conflict that will eventually cause a break in the relationship.[32] Independent women are stereotyped as usurping power and causing havoc in their households. Even more, independent women are thought to take over traditional male roles with the understanding that "if they can do things by themselves, then they don't need men." The underlying message is linked to traditional ideologies of women that place them in secondary and subservient roles to men. Thus, SAACW are not immune to the modern spinster motif and "Miss Independent" image that are reinforced in the Black church and society.

"I Choose—Single and Satisfied"

The image of the single and satisfied woman does not quite fit the social milieu of today. There are SAACW that are single because it's simply their choice. They are perceived as selfish and pathological because their independence is an affront to societal expectations and demands. *I choose, I enjoy my space, I love what I do, I love who I am, my life is full*, or *my life does not include a husband, maybe a boyfriend, maybe a sexual partner, maybe cohabitating with another person, but not a husband, it's not that I have any*

30. Ibid., 183.
31. Ibid.
32. Ibid., 184.

issues with men, I view my life and path differently. SAACW who fall in this category love their homes, work, social lives, friendships and families. People choose to ignore their self sufficiency because they truly believe that one day these women will eventually change their mind. *I choose* is a conflicting statement to speak publicly. However, their single and satisfied attitudes are disturbing to those who idealize coupled persons and denigrate single women. In contrast, it is even more perplexing for midlife women who do not view the continuation of their lives as one that includes marriage.

IN SUMMARY

In summary, there are many diverse cultural images of SAACW that are reinforced in the Black church and society. In general, African American women are placed in a precarious situation as they challenge some of the cultural images and myths that follow them. This chapter has examined some of the social commentary that is very controversial in many African American circles. Some believe that there is no validity to a male shortage hypothesis, while others believe that there is some truth in it. My point in this chapter has been to highlight some of the cultural and religious images that engender SAACW and to spark some conversation about the realities and myths that are prevalent in the African American community. SAACW have a unique place in the conversation as older seasoned women. Other sociocultural images, themes and concepts are examined in chapter 2 of the thematic narrative analysis. In chapter 7, I will further examine the damaging impact of cultural images and historical mythical images from a relational-cultural theory perspective.

Chapter 2

Thematic Narrative Analysis and Results of SAACW in Midlife

PURPOSE

This research serves as a platform to "privilege the voices,"[1] experiences and identities of three single African American women "Diane" (43), "Angie" (48) and "Tracy" (53). The experiences of these women are examined from their varied sociocultural narratives that are informed by their individual, communal and religious contexts. It is important in this research to explore the societal perceptions and projections from the cultural phenomena of singleness, midlife and African American women in the twenty-first century.

Data Gathering and Thematic Narrative Analysis

The data-gathering process involved in-depth interviews to ascertain the sociocultural narratives, histories and experiences of SAACW. I enlisted three African American women from different Christian communities, educational backgrounds and professional settings. I interviewed and taped the participants both individually and collectively using a questionnaire template as a guide for their responses. They were invited to share their experiences as single African American women and their beliefs about

---

1. Lartey, "Candler Cohort Group Meeting."

African American men in the context of the church and society. The audio-tapes were then transcribed and pseudonyms were assigned for anonymity. As a means of capturing the essence of their experiences in diverse settings and environments, pertinent themes were gathered and a thematic narrative analysis explored additional meanings from their narratives. Their sociocultural narratives are examined in this segment of the data analysis and serve as a response to the diverse images of SAACW in the Black church and society as explored in chapter 1. Other findings will be presented in subsequent chapters. The following section presents the research findings and results for SAACW.

SOCIOCULTURAL NARRATIVE RESULTS

Narratives of the Single Self-Identity

Question: What comes to mind when you think about your life as a single African American woman?

Although singleness is common in the twenty-first century, there are many societal messages and religious assumptions that are conveyed to SAACW. Because of commonly held beliefs about African American women's struggles to find suitable mates, it is necessary to understand an African American women's self-identity in terms and descriptions that are defined by them. Both within the African American community and beyond, African American women are defined in ways that deny their full humanity.

The first narrative summary that serves as an interpretive lens for SAACW is what I term *self-identity*. When asked, *What comes to mind when you think about your life as a single African American woman?* their responses included:

> Diane, age 43: It is a normal state of being and not an anomaly. It's just the way that it is. I don't think I look at it as if it is something wrong; it's just that I'm Black and single.

> Angie, age 48: I feel that I am blessed because I choose to see the glass half full instead of half empty. I'm blessed to be alive and living out my purpose as a pastor. I believe that singleness is the path chosen for me by God so I don't lament a lot over being single.

Tracy, age 53: I think of freedom with unlimited opportunities and no boundaries, freedom because I don't have the responsibility for family. I'm free to make choices that don't affect anyone but me. So with that freedom my opportunities for happiness are increased because I can explore different areas of interest and opportunity in my life.

Several themes were analyzed from this *Narrative of the Single Self-Identity*; these themes are: (1) *pathology*, (2) *vocation*, and (3) *freedom and choice*.

Theme of Pathology

Diane's *Narrative of the Single Self-Identity* explores the concept of pathology that is usually associated with single individuals.[2] The pathology that Diane experiences is that of an unmarried Black woman in the twenty-first century who has not fulfilled the role of marriage and family that the society has prescribed for her. Societal conventions suggest that Diane's pathology is threefold: she is *Black*, she is *single*, and she is *abnormal*. Yet, Diane contradicts and even challenges the societal conventions identifying herself as "Black and single," an identity that is healthy, normal and authentic.

Theme of Vocation

Likewise, Angie's single self-identity is greatly influenced by her vocational path in life. Her singleness and vocation as a pastor are paths chosen by God. *In Single Adults and the Life Cycle*, Berliner, Jacob, and Schwartzberg examine the traditional views of marriage as the next progressive path to adulthood in which "the single person may become frozen, waiting for marriage, not moving forward with the business of life."[3] Angie defies the

---

2. Schwartzberg et al., *Single in a Married World*, examines the problem of singlehood. Feeling "deviant" with regards to marital status creates an added burden. In response to societal and family pressure to marry and this sense of deviance, one may make marital status an organizing feature of one's life, and then view the rest of one's life through this lens. A standard of adult development that emphasizes marriage and a traditional family only reinforces marriage as a gate to adulthood and does little to inform us about what makes a good life for single people. This lack of information can make it difficult to move out of a reactive position to the "standard" and find a comfortable definition of self as a single person (5).

3. Ibid., 163.

traditional norms and has chosen to redefine her own status in life. Rather than lamenting a great deal over the fact that she is single at forty-eight years old, Angie is discovering how her singleness and her vocation as a pastor coincide in fulfilling her purpose in life. Angie acknowledges that life is seen through the lens of possibility or difficulty; however, she feels blessed with the possibilities set before her.

Theme of Freedom and Choice

Along the same lines, themes of freedom and choice are outlined in Tracy's *Narrative of the Single Self-Identity*. As a single woman, Tracy enjoys her freedom. Marriage and family require a different level of responsibility and dedication. In other words, marriage could possibly restrict her freedom and choices. Tracy knows that her singleness is dedicated to her own interests, needs, desires and passions. What makes her happy and the journey toward her happiness is what she seeks at this time in her life. Singleness is a period of time where she is not confined to one role, but has identified "unlimited opportunities" that are available to her as a single woman. Tracy has set the parameters of her own life as a single adult woman.

Thematic Narrative Analysis

In their *Narratives of the Single Self-Identity*, the participants describe their thoughts on singleness from sociocultural perspectives. The results indicate that a single self-identity is defined by the participants as an integration of their past and present life experiences, values and beliefs. Second, it is recognition of their personhood and character as African American women. Although they are single, they are not solely defined by their singleness. "That's just the way that it is"—Diane describes herself as a normal human being who embodies her singleness and takes pride in her Black heritage. Angie's singleness and vocation as a pastor complement each other to fulfill her purpose in life. She seems satisfied with the plans that God has set for her and feels "blessed" and "chosen" as a single woman. Tracy embodies her singleness because it affords her freedom, choices and opportunities that "increase her happiness." Their narratives indicate that a single self-identity is experienced and lived in a multiplicity of ways. Singleness seems empowering for these women as they have deliberately chosen their own paths to follow rather than traditional paths that have been set within the society.

Narratives of Society and African American Women

Question: What are some common perceptions and/or misperceptions that you have experienced in the society as a single African American woman?

African American women are perceived through many distorted images in the society. Despite the varied accomplishments of African American women that are prevalent, they continue to overcome oppression and denigration within the culture and society. Because of their race, gender, class and socioeconomic status, African American women face many unique challenges. Although they may share common realties with other women, their experiences and everyday lives are often misrepresented in contemporary culture more so than any other group of women. How the participants respond to these misrepresentations in the broader society is what I am calling the *Narratives of Society and African American Women*. There were diverse responses from the participants when asked about their perceptions of the society. Their responses included:

> Diane, age 43: Society doesn't value me. I'm a woman and I'm Black and they don't value either of those things. So I can't look at society to dictate to me being okay with myself because if I were to do that I would never be okay with my skin, I would never be okay with how I look, I would never be okay with who I am. I would always be striving to somehow fit in to what society says is valuable, beautiful, is worth love. I can't do that. I think the people that I have around me affirm me and I think growing up my maternal grandmother told me I was wonderful and I was so smart and pretty. She had me thinking I was Miss America. Growing up when other people didn't feel that way about me I took it like, "I feel bad about you I'm the bomb."

> Angie, age 48: I want to make sure that I challenge certain stereotypes about African American women and about women in the church in particular and certain notions in the culture and religion. First of all single life is not a death sentence. And you can have a fulfilled life as a single person. I have to challenge anything in terms of racism and sexism, those things that keep women in oppression. I feel compelled to challenge those notions.

Tracy, age 53: Negative. Their desire is to make me look other than positive. The very things that I should embrace, I do so constructively. I remember when the first lady appeared on the scene, Michelle Obama, everything was negative from her facial expressions or perceived as such. Not that she could be intense, not that her facial structure doesn't lend to a natural smile. Instead of her being quick and articulate, it was perceived that she was bitter and angry, so really it hasn't changed. I just feel like some of the perceptions that society has about me are arrived at through ignorance and not consistent with my experiences. I deliberately give my best anywhere that I am because the assumption is that I'm going to give something else and that's not my nature.

The prevailing themes in the *Narratives of Society and African American women* are: (1) *value*, (2) *challenge*, and (3) *inconsistency*.

Theme of Value

Diane reflects on the value placed on her gender as a female and her race as a Black person. For her, the society does not place any value on her race or gender. She has developed a positive sense of self and identity despite the "double jeopardy" that exists by virtue of her being Black and female. Relying on a strong ancestral connection with her maternal grandmother, Diane learned some valuable lessons about her worth in the world. She articulates what she finds most challenging about being a Black woman as she explains being "comfortable in her skin." Diane knows that she will never be able to "fit in" according to what society believes is "valuable, "beautiful" or "worth love." However, she draws on her own internal strengths rather than external voices that diminish her value and humanity.

Theme of Challenge

Angie challenges "certain notions" and "stereotypes" that oppress African American women in the church and society. In addition to racism and sexism, Angie discerns that "certain notions" about single people are inaccurate. "Single life is not a death sentence" and "single women can live fulfilled lives." Common myths about single women imply that their lives are stagnant because they are single. Other implications suggest that single women are unhappy or unsettled because they don't have what other married women have—a marriage, husband or children. This way of thinking along with other oppressive stereotypes about women is what Angie believes needs reproof and challenge in the church and society.

Theme of Inconsistency

Society's perceptions of Tracy are "negative or less than positive" and are based on "ignorant assumptions" instead of her experiences as an African American woman. The inconsistency that Tracy names calls into question her behavior in public settings and her personhood that she embraces "constructively." In other words, how she is perceived in the society raises so many questions. On a much larger stage, these same perceptions and public opinions about the first lady Michelle Obama are inconsistent. Assumptions about her "facial expressions" and perceived "attitude" are often criticized and deliberately misunderstood. Although Tracy and Michelle Obama have diverse socioeconomic backgrounds, marital status and philosophies in life, a divisive society is unmoved by their unique differences as African American women.

Thematic Narrative Analysis

The results in the *Narratives of Society and African American Women* describe the racial and sexual attitudes felt by those in the society. Although racial tensions have been longstanding in this country, the participants name the difficulty of living with these tensions. Diane and Tracy describe the misconceptions that often follow Black women in America. By virtue of being Black and female they represent two devalued groups in America. Conversely, Angie feels compelled to debunk many of the stereotypes and formulations that are specifically oppressive to African American women in America. What do their narratives reveal about the plight of both single and African American women in the society? It reveals that there is a dividing line where African American women are not embraced like their White female counterparts. Tracy makes the connecting point with her example of the first lady Michelle Obama. As an accomplished African American woman and first lady, she's had to defend herself publicly against the "angry Black woman stereotype."[4] Likewise, their narratives indicate that African

4. Snorton, in "What About Those Angry Black Women," states that the "angry Black woman" is a force to be reckoned with or, better yet, avoided. In the African American community, she is known as "b–t–h" (207).

American women are placed in a position where they have to justify and qualify their existence in the world. Diane states that "I'm the bomb," an urban description that means, "I'm the best." Angie says, "My life, my singleness is not a death sentence." Tracy states, "I deliberately give my best wherever I go because that's my nature." Their narratives indicate that there is more depth and meaning in the lives of African American women; however, bridging this understanding with an indifferent society is a complex venture.

Narratives of the Black Church and Singleness

Question: How does your church affiliation support you as a single African American woman?

The Black church has historically been a strong spiritual and religious support for the African American community. Like all churches across all demographic lines, the Black church has large percentages of women who "dominate not only in membership but in fundraising and organizing activities."[5] Hence, the focus in this discussion is to discover how the Black church supports SAACW and what messages, images and perceptions are circulated in this environment. Although the Black church is a communal space made up of diverse families, how friendly and receptive is this environment to the multitudes of single African American women that attend church each Sunday and are functioning members? The *Narratives of the Black Church and Singleness* examines the community called the Black church. When asked about the *support of their church affiliation* their responses included:

> Diane, age 43: I don't think the church is supportive. I can't tell you how many times people in church say very hurtful things and if you are not fortified inside you could get offended. I had people in church say what's "wrong with you why are you not married? You don't have kids what's wrong with you, how old are you? Old maid? We have to find you a husband; we have to pray for you to find a husband." I'm like really. I've had people give a prophecy to me that I was single because I wanted a husband that was going to be spectacular and that I would have to deal with the fact that my husband may be average run of the mill, everyday Joe. I'm like okay this is what God told you, God didn't tell me anything

5. Day, *Unfinished Business*," 16.

like that. Like I wouldn't want the guy directing traffic out in the church parking lot—they say that's why I'm single. That's funny I would think God would tell me too.

Angie, age 48: The church views single women with suspicion. The notion that single women, especially pastors think that you are either a lesbian and I think at this point it's nothing wrong with that. But they think you are a lesbian because you are not married. Or that you are trying to take someone's husband or that you are after someone's husband. It's got to be, you are not married or you have something to hide. Singleness can't be the reason that you are not married, there has to be a reason, it has to be a sinister reason.

Tracy, age 53: I don't believe that my specific church provides a specific ministry that addresses my singleness. That's not an indictment, although it should, they don't know what to do with it. They don't know what to do with people that are single because they don't really hear in the Bible about many single people obviously Paul was and Paul was strange and he was different, but we never talk about Paul and his singleness. In fact we feel that Paul was able to do all that he was able to do because he was single. But we don't talk about his singleness, we acknowledge that he was, but we don't talk about it, so the church doesn't know what to do.

Three emergent themes are explored in the *Narratives of the Black Church and Singleness:* (1) *church hurt,* (2) *reasoning,* and (3) *"Paul."*

Theme of Church Hurt

Diane has been the recipient of many hurtful comments made by some of the people in her church community. Church members have made statements about her age, calling her an "old maid." They have "prayed for her to find a husband" while at the same time prophesying or chastising her for wanting a "spectacular husband" rather than an "average husband." The attitudes and beliefs of some of the church members has been a frustrating space for Diane. Having to brace herself against the barrage of negative attacks speaks to the level of discomfort that she experiences. God is used as the catalyst to substantiate their claims about her not having a husband. However, Diane challenges what they have been told by God versus what she hears from God herself.

Theme of Reasoning

Angie's church denomination is very suspicious of single women. Because the majority of churches are made up of women, single women often find themselves in a precarious predicament with married women. Not all married women are acceptable or comfortable with single women in close proximity of their husbands. They fear that single women are "after their husbands." Others, including some pastors, shame single women with labels such as "lesbian." "Singleness can't be the reason that you are not married, there has to be a reason, and it's a sinister reason." Her narrative addresses how the character and motives of single African American women are often questioned by those in the church. The reasoning that goes on in the minds of church members is unfathomable.

Theme of "Paul"

Tracy points out the predicament that most churches face in the twenty-first century. How does the church minister to such a large demographic of single women that attend church each Sunday? Paul is the quintessential model for singleness in the New Testament and Tracy's analogy of Paul is that he is a single person who is "strange" and "different." Paul was able to accomplish so much in ministry because he was allegedly single. However, the general misconception about single people is that they have more time to give to work, church and their families than married people. On some level, Tracy feels out of place, "strange" and "different," like Paul.

Thematic Narrative Analysis

The *Narratives of the Black Church and Singleness* explores the reactions of the participants in their various communities of faith. The three participants are unanimous in their perceptions about the churches where they worship. The results indicate that although they attend different Black protestant churches, some of the perceptions about single women are similar. These perceptions are applicable to the "Black church"; however, it may indicate that churches with other ethnic demographics have similar issues with locating single women. Moreover, their narratives suggest that the Black church holds embedded beliefs about marriage and singleness. Church parishioners are adamant in Diane's narrative that "she needs a husband." Likewise, Angie's church denomination believes that if "she is not married then she has something to hide." The embedded beliefs that are upheld by the Black church also indicate that there is a disconnection in the way that it does not address or "doesn't even know how to address" the specific concerns of single African American women. Tracy desires some biblical or spiritual guidance for her specific needs as a single woman; however, her needs for ministry in this area are overlooked. More importantly, their narratives reveal how the church has been inhospitable at times to single African American women who have decided to remain single for one reason or another. Instead they have chosen not to conform to the pressures of marriage and the nuclear family despite what others have said or perceived about them.

Narratives of the African American Male Shortage

Question: What comes to mind when you hear the statement, "There is a shortage of good African American men?"

A major impetus for this study includes the reactions and thoughts of the participants as it relates to partnering with African American men. According to Ralph Richard Banks, "Black women of all socioeconomic classes remain single in part because the ranks of Black men have been decimated by incarceration, educational failure, and economic disadvantage."[6]

With that being said about the caliber of African American men that are available to African American women, it is necessary to identify how this cultural phenomenon impacts their marital status and what deeper questions they may have as a result of this. When asked about the statement, *What comes to mind when you hear the statement, "There is a shortage of good African American men?"* their responses included:

> Diane, age 43: I think there are good and bad men of all colors. It's really based on the person. I don't believe in the Black men shortage, I don't believe any of that. I feel like if I'm meant to be with someone, I will. To me that's where my faith kicks in. God to me can transcend any circumstance of what it looks like in the flesh. So if I believe that he is a healer or I believe that if I'm meant to be with someone or meet someone, I will. I don't cut God off when it comes to that part of my life. I don't say there is a shortage, or there are a lot of Black men in jail or gay, that could be anyone. That to me can deter what God can do.

6. Ibid., 2.

Angie, age 48: I get tired of that statement but at the same time it may be true if you are talking about educated African American women who are seeking educated African American men because I think the statistics support that. There are more women than men. However, I think sometimes that statement causes a lot of grief and tension and can be unfair to African American men sometimes. The question really requires a deeper analysis. At the end of the day the questions we should be asking are what types of African American men and women are seeking relationships? What are they seeking and where are they seeking them? What targets are you seeking? What are you trying to do in the search? Is it marriage ultimately or is it having a relationship or just kicking it? What are you going to do after you've found this person? So I think it requires us to do some deeper thinking and do deeper analysis of what we are trying to do.

Tracy, age 53: Well I believe the statistics that tell us about the number of men who are in prison, African American men who are gay or homosexual, but I also believe that of the ones who don't fit in those two categories that they are not necessarily educationally or financially compatible to most of the women that remain and are single for whatever reason. There is some truth to that statement. It doesn't leave one hopeless, it doesn't leave me hopeless that the possibilities of finding an African American man are impossible, doesn't make me feel like it's impossible. But at the same time it could mean because God has not ordered my path and that I haven't met many men who are compatible, who are not intimidated, or that there may be men of different races that may be available. I am open to that.

Several themes are pertinent to the *Narratives of the African American Male Shortage.* These themes are: (1) *doubt*, (2) *relational analysis*, and (3) *compatibility.*

Theme of Skepticism

Diane names her skepticism in a male shortage and in the percentages of African American men who are incarcerated or gay. From her perspective, African American men are not the presenting problem and there is no phenomenon to suggest there is a male shortage. In fact, the opposite is true. Although negative comments have been stated about African American men, Diane believes that there are African American men to date or marry. She also believes that all men have good and bad qualities. As she stated, "It depends on the person" and she is willing to date African American men. She is also willing to allow God's will to manifest in her dating life. Some of her embedded beliefs indicate that the power of words and negative rhetoric about African American men can potentially advance or hinder God's work in her relationship life.

Theme of Relational (Deeper) Analysis

In contrast, Angie believes that there is some truth in the African American male shortage claim, particularly if you examine the female-to-male ratio of educated African Americans.[7] Yet, this truth does not minimize some of the tension and grief that is evident in making this claim. On the one hand statistical claims support this; on the other hand these claims are unfair to African American men. Thus, the two paradoxical natures require a deeper analysis and conversation. The analysis examines: (1) *the types of African American men and women who are seeking relationships and* (2) *the quality of relationships that are transpiring among them.* People partner, date or marry for different reasons and Angie's critical analysis suggests that more thought needs to be given in this process. All dating does not lead to marriage; therefore those seeking should explore their own desires in this matter. Angie's pastoral analysis moves beyond a male shortage and over-romanticizing companionship. Her analysis reveals the power dynamics and negotiation that transpires between individuals as they explore the boundaries and exclusivity within the relationship. The challenge lies in reflecting on the needs of those seeking long-term relationships.

Theme of Compatibility

Relationship compatibility is a controversial topic in the African American community. Successful African American women are seeking successful

---

7. According to the *Journal of Blacks in Higher Education*, Black women hold a large lead over Black men in almost every facet of higher education. Black women currently earn about two-thirds of all African American bachelor's degree awards, 70 percent of all master's degrees, and more than 60 percent of all doctorates. Black women also hold a majority of all African American enrollments in law, medical, and dental schools. See the *Journal of Blacks in Higher Education* 51 (2006), http://www.jbhe.com/news_views/51_index.html.

African American men who have comparable education and financial stability. Tracy's theme of compatibility names the sobering reality of high incarceration rates, homosexuality, educational failure, financial compatibility, and intimidation that make dating opportunities and long-term relationships difficult for single African American women. Tracy admits to wanting companionship with successful African American men; however, if this does not materialize, she is open to dating outside of her race.

Thematic Narrative Analysis

There were mixed reviews of the *Narratives of the African American Male Shortage*. First, the male shortage is negative rhetoric or unfair to African American men as stipulated in both Diane's and Angie's narrative. Second, educational failure is a main contributor to the male shortage as identified in Angie's and Tracy's narrative. Tracy adds high incarceration rates, homosexuality, financial compatibility and intimidation. In some ways, Tracy feels that African American men are intimidated or perceive African American women as unapproachable and this could contribute to a male shortage. In contrast, Angie's narrative opens the door for conversation and dialogue on relational factors that threaten dating opportunities and long-term relationships between African American men and women. Angie connected her understanding of a male shortage to a relational analysis and challenge for those who are seeking relationships. It's one matter to seek companionship; however, it's an entirely different matter to maintain a healthy and cordial relationship. Overall, the participants were not discouraged from partnering with African American men. However, one participant, Tracy, was not opposed to availing herself to other dating opportunities in the event that she could not find compatible relationships with African American men. Her narrative best sums up the duality of wanting companionship with African American men, but having to look outside of her normal parameters for companionship.

In addition to factors that impact compatibility, both Diane and Tracy discuss God's role in their relationship status. Three images of God are illustrated from their narrative summaries:

1. *God as transcendent*: Diane states, "God can transcend any circumstance of what it looks like in the flesh." If she is designated to meet

someone, nothing can prevent her from meeting the right person when God ordains it. Her faith and God's transcendent power exceeds it all.

2. *God as healer*: Just as Diane is confident that God is a healer, she is confident that God is able to attend to her in times of need. God is involved in all aspects of her life.

3. *God orders the path*: Tracy states, "God has not ordered my path." In this instance she speaks about remaining hopeful of meeting an African American man; however, she believes that she has not met "the one" because God has not ordered her path to meet him at this time. At the right time God orchestrates who she meets and how she meets the right man.

Narratives of Dating African American Men

Question: What have your past relationships been like with African American men?

To build further on the image of African American men, it is important to this research to give insight on the experiences of SAACW in the context of dating African American men in intimate and personal settings. When asked the question, *What have your past dating relationships been like with African American men?* their responses included:

> Diane, age 43: Some have been good, some have been bad. But when I think of the ones that were bad, it was more than the person being a bad person it was really me wanting that person to help fulfill me. And no human can do that. I was coming at the relationship in that way—thinking that the person was going to give me fulfillment and complete me. When you are looking for someone to validate who you are as a person, you will deal with things differently. Things do happen; it's not all the person's fault. It is the position that you gave the person in your life.

> Angie, age 48: To be honest with you nonexistent. The few relationships that I've had, it's been an emotional tug of war. They wanted absolute control and I wasn't going to relinquish that. I'm the kind of person that if I've been slighted in any way, I'm going to get you back—not violently, not physically but with my speech, my actions, I'll get you back in some kind of way. Once I lose respect

for a person, the respect for me is gone and I just can't seem to find that respect and trust again. I've dated two men and it's been 12 years between the two.

Tracy, age 53: Varied, generally I have given more than I received, to the extent we are not together because I couldn't give anymore or it was one sided. I didn't limit myself to men who were my equals or who had the same experiences educationally, financially or professionally. I didn't limit myself to that group. With that, I was often able to give more than some of the men I've dated. Some of the relationships have been one sided. Additionally, I allowed myself to be in relationships that were draining or sexually oriented as opposed to the relationships having some substance. I have compromised myself for what I really wanted. I wanted a healthy relationship, but I compromised for the sake of being in relationship and allowed and tolerated more than I should have. I have been abused in two relationships in my life. My perception of Black men as a whole, I equated it to who they are versus who all Black men are.

Several themes are explored in the *Narratives of Dating African American Men*: (1) *validation*, (2) *emotional imbalance*, and (3) *compromise*.

Theme of Validation

Diane's past relationships with African American men have been good and bad. Of the ones that were bad, Diane accepts responsibility for her personal needs of validation that resulted in the demise of her relationships. Ironically, she doesn't believe her past dating partners were bad individuals. However, she makes the correlation that her own insecurities blinded her in her past relationships. The men in her past dating life had needs of their own; however, Diane was unable to reciprocate their needs in the relationship. Diane now knows that "no human being" could possibly complete her. Clearly, how she understood her needs of acceptance caused some friction in her past dating relationships with African American men.

Theme of Emotional Imbalance and Control

Angie has not been in many relationships with African American men. Within the past twelve years she has been in two relationships. She describes her past relationships as an "emotional tug of war" in which her partners were determined to control her; however, Angie refused to relinquish her power. In their attempts to control her, Angie lost respect and trust in her relationships. It is obvious that Angie felt very strongly about how these men asserted themselves in the relationship. Her feelings of anger, pain, betrayal, resentment and revenge are evident as she recalls her story. The twelve-year span between the two relationships suggests the emotional toll and the years it took to rebuild her confidence.

Theme of Compromise

Tracy's past relationships with African American men have been very "one sided." From her own admission, Tracy takes responsibility for deliberately placing herself in compromising positions in which she "tolerated more than she should have." Although she desired a "healthy relationship," she compromised herself for the "sake of being in relationship," to the extent that she was abused twice. Tracy made some unhealthy choices in her previous relationships and put herself in harm's way. Tracy has learned that she dealt with certain "Black men" with questionable character. However, this behavior is not representative of all "Black men as a whole."

Thematic Narrative Analysis

The *Narratives of Dating African American Men* revealed that the participants had both positive and negative reactions when dating African American men. During the course of their dating relationships, there were factors such as acceptance, control, trust and compromise that ultimately caused friction in how they related with one another. Looking back, Diane, Angie and Tracy realized that they needed their relationships to validate them in some way. Diane wanted her relationships to complete her. Tracy wanted her relationships "for the sake of being in relationship." However, Angie required a different validation. She wanted a partner that would equitably honor her place and voice in the relationship. The research reveals that there were positive and negative expectations on the part of the men and participants. Their relationships dissolved because of the negative tensions that festered over time. Ultimately, these negative tensions are what drove them apart. Both parties bear some responsibility in how their issues were negotiated during the course of their dating relationships. Dating was not as enjoyable in this case because of the tensions and unrealistic expectations on both parts. Out of the three participants, only Diane reported some "good" dating experiences with African American men. Angie's past dating experiences were "controlling" while Tracy's were both sexually and physically draining. Diane and Tracy were clear that they had certain self-esteem issues. Thus, dating in this narrative is not just reflective of the tensions that exist within African American men, but also the tensions that exist within African American women, as well.

IMPLICATIONS OF THE ANALYSIS

In conclusion, the thematic narrative analysis is based upon the firsthand accounts of the sociocultural realities of SAACW. Themes such as self-identity, African American womanhood, African American manhood, dating and the Black church were examined in this research. It is my intent that this thematic narrative analysis will invite more in-depth dialogue about the identities that are intrinsic to single women and SAACW. The narratives of the women in this study gave a clear representation of the multifaceted ways in which they are viewed in the culture and society.

Chapter 3

"I Think Often about What's Going to Happen as I Grow Older"

THE MIDLIFE JOURNEY

Midlife is a natural transition that all women face during their lifetime. It is a period where one begins to see oneself more clearly. It's a time to find meaning, purpose and to discover the true and authentic self. However, many emotional concerns emerge during this phase because it is a complex journey that impacts women of all ethnicities. Several narratives from the perspective of SAACW are explored with this understanding in mind. Having reached a midlife milestone, they share their outlook on life from several narratives: *Midlife and Change, Loneliness-Aloneness-Regret, Work, Singleness and Growing Older.* There are a range of emotions, experiences and culminating events that have brought them to this point in time. Many existential concerns about the meaning of life without a partner, marriage or children are raised; however, how this is translated within their familial, social and religious circles is significant. Although the term "midlife crisis" is a cultural phenomenon in which women who do struggle during this time are relegated to "acting out" driven by fears of being over the hill, midlife can also mark a season of challenge, reflection, renewal and growth as evident in their stories.[1] They experience midlife not as the

---

1. Borysenko, *Woman's Book of Life*, 143.

beginning of the end, but as a time of great possibilities, longings, regrets and coming into their own.

Natalie Schwartzberg, Kathy Berliner and Demaris Jacob, in *Single in a Married World: A Life Cycle Framework for Working with the Unmarried Adult*, examine the emotional issues and therapeutic responses of the midlife phase for the single adult in their forties to mid-fifties. This midlife phase "represents a critical time of taking stock, of reshaping and rethinking one's place in the world."[2] The authors posit that during this midlife phase several emotional processes emerge for both single men and women with the weight of closing options falling hardiest on single women.[3] The emotional process for the single adult in their forties to mid-fifties is:

1. Addressing the fantasy of the ideal American family,
   a. accepting the possibility of never marrying
   b. accepting the possibility of not having own biological children

2. Defining the meaning of work current and future,

3. Defining an authentic life for oneself that can be accomplished within the single status, and

4. Defining an authentic life as an aging adult.[4]

These authors also give valuable insight on the life cycle development of the single adult from multilayered perspectives of the single person and the family. Moreover, their premise supports cultural, racial and gender-related differences in conjunction to the life cycle framework.[5]

ADDRESSING THE "IDEAL" FAMILY FANTASY

Single women in their forties and fifties have certain idyllic understandings about marriage, family and children. Those who have reached this midlife juncture are increasingly aware of long standing beliefs from their families, churches and society about the sanctity of marriage and family. Beliefs about what it means to be male or female and wife or husband are deeply rooted in the culture. However, no matter how well one has prepared mentally, emotionally or spiritually or what positive affirmations are cultivated

2. Ibid., 82.
3. Ibid.
4. Ibid., 56.
5. Ibid., 52.

from within, there still are "unilateral messages in our society that make marriage the only sane goal for the mentally healthy adult."[6] When societal expectations for marriage are not met then some plausible explanation is demanded by friends, family or church members. "For women, these explanations tend to be more deficient-based (e.g., some basic personality flaw) or blaming (e.g., my mother didn't provide a good role model.)"[7] As noted by Schwartzberg, Berliner and Jacob, the society plays a major role in validating or invalidating singleness as a normative status. Ultimately, when singleness becomes a normative means of "being" and "living" then and only then has it reached an acceptable and authentic place in society.[8] The ideal family fantasy is discussed in what I term the *Narratives of Midlife and Change* where Diane, Angie and Tracy discuss their thoughts on marriage and family from earlier recollections in their twenties.

Narratives of Midlife and Change

Diane, age 43: I feel weird because when I think about my life in my teens and twenties, I didn't really picture myself being single and not having children. It was an automatic assumption that by the time I was in my forties I would have those things. For me not to have those things it's kind of weird that I have to see my life in a way that I never really thought about.

Angie, age 48: I'm happy, happy to be living. Every day that I can wake up that means that there is still a chance to walk in God's purpose and get better. Hopefully, as I've gotten older, I'm wiser so my decision making is better. In my twenties, I was looking at the lens very differently. I had set in my mind that I would be married with a kid that was the goal. So I look forward to everyday as it comes. I'm just happy that I'm living and among the living.

Tracy, age 53: Excited honestly, excited about being in my fifties. If you had asked me in my twenties what my fifties would look like this is not what I imagined. In my twenties I thought about husband, children and probably around now grandchildren maybe. I thought about success even though I didn't know what that was

6. Ibid., 84.
7. Ibid.
8. Ibid.

going to look like—more established of the societal norm, marriage, children, house, and two car garages. I feel because my life has unfolded in the way that it has, I'm excited because there are no children, there is no husband, no family, no house and 2.5 cars and there's not retirement plan and vacation, none of those things I thought I could not live without. And I'm happy, I really am. I started a new journey in my life with regards to school, to fleshing out the vision that I feel God has given me and that's my baby, that's what matters most to me right now. As far as my career is concerned, I'm very happy where I am right now.

There are several insights that these women reveal in examining the ideal family fantasy. Having reached and surpassed their fortieth birthdays, Diane, Angie and Tracy envisioned their lives much differently as young adult African American women. Naturally, their belief systems were very similar to the cultural assumptions for marriage and family. For example, it was an obvious disappointment for Diane not meeting her desired goal for marriage and family. She assumed that her aspirations for this would automatically fall in place; however, now it feels strange, unsettling and "weird" to think about her life in a way that she didn't envision or contemplate. As she stated, "For me not having those things [husband and children] it's kind of weird that I have to see my life in a way I never really thought about." This conversation invited her to explore her beliefs in light of her fears and to examine her footing in the world as a single African American woman. It also challenges her to think about her life differently as she grapples with this new way of thinking and being that may not include a husband or children. Letting go of the dream is certainly a reality that she may face.

While, Diane felt strange in reflecting on her aspirations for marriage and family, Angie and Tracy felt "happy" and "excited" in approaching midlife without the typical lives that they imagined. Addressing the "ideal" family means positioning themselves for the next chapter in their lives beyond marriage and family. Although neither of these women fulfilled their aspirations for marriage and family, they have chosen to redirect their energies in pursuing other interests, goals and adventures. They feel fortunate and passionate about living a quality of life on their own terms. For example, Angie hopes to make "wise" choices and decisions in this next phase of her life. Tracy, on the other hand, focuses on a new "journey" toward pursuing an academic degree. Diane, Angie and Tracy have approached their midlife season with the understanding that certain "ideals" for marriage and family did not materialize. However, finding their "legitimate space in the society" as unmarried women and the cultural realties, changes, shifts and reactions this brings about is important in the therapeutic setting for single women.[9]

Diane, Angie and Tracy now face what is called *watching the closing doors* in which the possibility of never marrying or having biological children is realized.[10] As suggested by Schwartzberg, Berliner and Jacob, women may feel like time is running out. The therapeutic implications denote that "feelings around marriage, and especially feelings around motherhood, will continue to recycle in lessening degrees of intensity throughout one's forties."[11] This is further described in what can be described as the *Narratives of Midlife Loneliness, Aloneness and Regret*.

Narratives of Midlife, Loneliness, Aloneness and Regret

Diane, age 43: It's loneliness. I always seem to have some doctor issue, so I've had surgery on my arm. I had a tumor, I went and had surgery. My god sister brought me home and then she left. I was in bed with my cast on my arm. I was really wishing someone was here just to sit and talk to me, help me. So the emotion that pops up for me is loneliness because I have to go through things alone a lot of the time. And sometimes I would prefer to go through things with someone and not just by myself or with my girlfriends. That pops up. It's when I'm wishing someone else was there to be with me in whatever the process is and it comes up for me a lot during those times. It's like when you are doing things and you wish someone else was there so that you could share that experience with them. It's such a cool experience that you wish you had a boyfriend or husband because he could do this with you, like this would be cool and wishing someone else was there while you are doing it and discovering it together and not just me.

Angie, age 48: My biggest regret is not having children. I always wanted to be a mother way more than I wanted to be a wife. When I told this to a girlfriend and she said wait a minute get that order right. Since I know that opportunity is slipping past me, I just haven't worried about it and I think this is the life that is set for me. Family babysitting is when those emotions come up. It's usually when I'm around children especially babies. I think about what

9. Ibid.
10. Ibid.
11. Ibid.

it would be like to have children, but a little bit of baby time with my nieces, nephews and cousins after a long weekend of that, I'm ready to give them back. I can always give them back.

Tracy, age 53: Aloneness and not having a significant other to share my life. Sometimes as women we need to talk it out, we need to work it out and I don't always have the luxury of being able to talk it out or work it out with anybody. Then enters God, I just have conversations with him, not that that's a bad thing but sometimes, I want to be held and I want someone to wipe my tears and I don't have that. It's happy times, success and painful times, difficulty in life, stressful times. So everything reminds me that I'm alone. I don't think that we are meant to be alone. Obviously God didn't think so either, God created the female to be that support and comfort for Adam. Adam was lonely; I don't think in my singleness I'm any different than Adam. To deny this is unrealistic. I think some of us have better coping mechanisms and live with it at different levels with different levels of comfort. Physically not having anyone in that space, physically not sharing space is to be alone. Loneliness is feeling like no one can ever be in that space.

Loneliness, aloneness and regret are natural emotional responses for single women. It is a challenge in those areas of life in which one is expected to have a family to call their own or where one is expected to have an escort for formal functions, social events and family gatherings. Although Diane, Angie and Tracy have expressed their empowerment as single women, there are moments when a more permanent connection is desired via a husband or children.

Diane recalls her feelings of sadness during her convalescence from surgery. Although she valued the support from her god sister during her recovery, she wanted a more intimate and permanent connection with a boyfriend or husband. Without ignoring the fact that women experience intimacy in many relationships and that girlfriend networks are alternative forms of security, support and intimacy, these support networks are not the only relational support that is desired. Diane's "loneliness" stems from wanting a deeper connection and a balance between spending time with her girlfriends versus the intimacy she wants to share with a boyfriend or husband. Furthermore, she desires to share her experiences, new adventures and intimacy with a designated person of her choice. Diane makes the distinction between the emotional support with her girlfriends versus the companionship and intimacy that she longs to share with a boyfriend or husband. These two dichotomies evoke different feelings for her. "Intimacy is designating the person or thing that is innermost, most familiar, or internal—in a relationship it marks one most closely associated or acquainted."[12]

The need for intimacy is further detailed in Tracy's narrative. At times, she desires a close and significant person to share her life. Her feelings of "aloneness" are felt most when she needs to "talk," "work things out" or "she wants to be held"; however, physically not having anyone to share her space feels isolating and lonely. Everything in her world including her successes, failures and difficulties in life are amplified and reminds her that she is a single woman who lives alone and is unmarried. In those moments, she prays to assuage some of the grief and tears that accompany her aloneness. God supported Adam during his season of loneliness, but will God do the same for her? Are her feelings important to God? Although she has her conversations and prayer time with God sometimes this is not enough when she desires physical intimacy, even sexual intimacy with a partner. Interestingly, Tracy provides her own working definitions of loneliness and aloneness. "Loneliness" in her estimation is a permanent feeling in which there is no hope or possibility of someone ever sharing her space. While "aloneness" is more of a transient feeling in which there is no one physically present at the moment to share her space, it does not rule out the possibility that someone can potentially fill that space. How she balances these emotions and her level of comfort is difficult for her.

Facing the possibility of never marrying or having children does raise feelings of "regret." The regret has to do with feeling a sense of loss and disappointment. Not all women desire husbands or boyfriends, but some may feel that they have missed opportunities for having children or experiencing motherhood. As a single woman who has reached midlife and her "procreative time limit," Angie now faces her disappointment and regret over the fact that physically time is an issue in regards to her having children.[13] She asserts that motherhood was much more important to her than fulfilling the role of a wife. Motherhood without the confines of marriage carries certain social stigmas against women who choose to parent in nontraditional settings. This is proven as Angie's friend states "get the order right." Women are expected to have a certain "order" in which they parent children and it is usually with a spouse. However, Angie has her own order and way of thinking that challenges the "proper order" as set by the larger

12. Madden, "Intimacy and Distance," 594.
13. Ibid.

society and culture. Angie doesn't mention other alternatives like adoption or surrogacy that are available for her. Nonetheless, she has learned to nurture and "deepen the available relationships with children" in her own familial unit to ease some of her longings for motherhood.[14] Sharing the responsibility of raising children is not always perfect and ideal because motherhood even by proxy requires energy, devotion and hard work.

In addressing the ideal family fantasy, there are many honest and raw emotions that impact midlife women who live alone without traditional families of their own. Midlife without the mandate of marriage feels weird but also represents a happy and exciting time of reflection and challenge. On the other hand, living alone sometimes is not a pleasant experience and Diane, Angie and Tracy were susceptible to feeling lonely, alone and moments of regret. Schwartzberg, Berliner and Jacob suggest several therapeutic methodologies for therapists in their work with helping single women to address marriage, motherhood and the "ideal" family fantasy. "The therapist must:

1. listen carefully to their explanations and not reframe them away,
2. allow room for the full expression of the feelings involved, and
3. give permission for the exploration of the range of choices that are still available."[15]

This is a prime opportunity for Diane, Angie and Tracy to explore where they are in life while managing their emotions.

DEFINING THE MEANING OF WORK, CURRENT AND FUTURE

The workplace provides emotional support, value, inspiration as well as challenge for midlife single women. Because midlife is a transition in which many questions surface, the workplace often gives personal meaning to women without families or children. "Personal meaning comes in many forms including pride in earning one's living, giving to society, creating something enduring and building a sense of power."[16] Work means more

14. Ibid., 87.
15. Ibid.
16. Ibid., 89.

than earnings; it is using skills, gifts, talents and abilities.[17] Creating a business, volunteering, mentoring, church ministry, leadership opportunities, or going back to school are ways in which midlife women can maximize their talents, gifts and abilities. One of the gifts of singleness is the freedom to explore other career avenues without the confines of a marriage, husband or children. Financial shifts and changes are explored without the worry of offsetting the marriage or family unit. Finding a meaningful and suitable work life for women involves compromise and honesty about specific work aspirations and future employment. This is further explained in Diane, Angie and Tracy's *Narratives of Midlife and Work*.

Narratives of Midlife and Work

> Diane, age 43: I don't like my career field as a paralegal but it's something that I know how to do very well. But I don't like it, in the future I hope to be doing something more fulfilling and that matches my gifts and talents. I can do my job because I'm smart but I feel nothing for the work. It's kind of like being this hollow dead person that comes in, does everything but I really don't like it. I want to help people. My ideal job would be working in a nonprofit and helping to raise money for different causes. If that means I go to different corporations and try to get money; I would do that corporate part, but anything that's helping people. Raising money for charity organizing people, I'm very detailed oriented, if you give me a box of papers. I will put some order to it. Organizing things for people, project manager anything like that, I'm good at that and I enjoy it. I have a friend who has an adolescent charity for young girls ages 13 to 18 called the Cobb county cuties, and I work with her. I like to give money to Doctors without Borders where these doctors fly to 3rd world countries and they do surgery, fix cleft palate, healers that go around world. Those are the only two things that I'm involved in.

> Angie, age 48: I'm actually looking for other opportunities because I like what I do as a researcher, but I always want to be growing and challenged and learn new things. I'm feeling kind of stuck right now because I'm not doing what I need to do on that end. I'm still trying to figure out what I want to do when I grow up. I'm in ministry as a pastor and doing so many things at one time.

17. Ibid.

I know ultimately I want to be where I am helping people and so I know I will be in ministry in some capacity. I want to further my education; I'm tired and burnt out. I know at some point I going to be pursuing doctoral studies somewhere. Right now I'm trying to figure out because I have so many interests.

Tracy, age 53: My work as a project consultant affords me an opportunity to engage, be creative, to be productive, and to contribute to life. It affords me an opportunity of ministry and life. I can't sit back and reflect all day as much as I would like to.

Assessing one's place in the workplace and evaluating one's life goals for employment is essential. There are many internal barometers that are indicative of one's passion, fulfillment or unfulfillment for a particular vocation or workplace. Diane doesn't like her current job because it makes her feel like a "hollow dead person." Although she is very proficient as a paralegal and has been actively engaged in this type of work for quite some time, it does not give her the sense of identity, purpose, value or meaning that she experiences with her charitable work and humanitarian contributions.

The sense of identity, purpose, value and meaning is also described in Angie's and Tracy's narratives. Angie is a researcher and pastor. She enjoys her work as a researcher, but "feels stuck" and envisions a new direction in her work life. Angie is still figuring out how to integrate all of her various interests, ministry and academic pursuits. Four factors are a source of inspiration for her in the workplace: "growth," "challenge," "learning new things" and "helping people." Similarly, Tracy's work as a project consultant is very rewarding because it affords her many opportunities of "creativity" and connection. She is inspired in a setting where she makes many "contributions towards life and ministry."

In contrast, there are diverse changes that take place in the workplace that make reevaluating career goals a necessity. Goals that were a set priority in earlier years are an entirely different set of goals in midlife.[18] Diane, Angie and Tracy feel that their career goals and ambitions have changed now that they are older. What seemed gratifying in their twenties has evolved to an entirely different set of values in their forties and fifties. They are now in a position to set new career goals. In midlife, "one can either solidify or reshape the personal meaning of one's current profession or begin

18. Ibid., 90.

the thinking and visualizing that precedes planning another life work."[19] Hence, this is a critical time to think about other skill sets, abilities and professional development that can enhance this new direction and focus in life.

DEFINING AN AUTHENTIC LIFE AS A SINGLE ADULT

Living an authentic, complete and satisfying single life means "not feeling that one's life is an imitation, that 'real' life is being lived by those married and/ or with children."[20] There are many misconceptions about African American women and the marriage controversy. According to these notions that are presented in popular culture, African American women have a difficult time finding mates for marital relationships. As a result, single African American women have an added pressure to live authentically in a society that often criticizes their marital status along with issues of race, gender and class. How one chooses to embrace singleness is a matter of choice. Some may fixate on this issue while others may not. Some may even enjoy the benefits and perks of remaining single. Still, others may find themselves vacillating between numerous positions as single women. "Seeing one's life as authentic does not necessarily mean giving up the idea of being married; it means giving up waiting to be married for real life to begin."[21]

My interviewees' *Narratives of Midlife and Singleness* explores the area of authenticity and singleness.

Narratives of Midlife and Singleness

> Diane, age 43: This is me and my life. I choose to celebrate it and live it regardless if there are good attributes or bad attributes. I never want to spend time wishing that I was something other than what I am. Then I'm missing my life.

> Angie, age 48: I like being single, I think the primary reason is that when it comes to major life decisions or something minor as trying to decide what to eat for dinner, I don't have to consult a soul. It's just me. I'm the type of person who likes to be around people but also crave solitude. At some point people just wear me

19. Ibid.
20. Ibid.
21. Ibid.

out and I just love church but sometimes I have to get away and I know that I can get away in my house.

Tracy, age 53: I know that there is more, more to experience if I had an opportunity to share it with someone.

Diane "celebrates" her accomplishments as a single woman. Rather than wishing she were married or imitating someone else's life, Diane embraces a life that she is feels good about. As well, Angie enjoys the perks as a single woman because she is free to make decisions that impact only her. She is truthful about her time and what she can give to those around her. Remarkably, she cherishes moments of solitude away from people in the privacy of her home where she spends quiet reflective time.

In addition, Tracy's authentic life is one where she desires to share "more" of her experiences along her journey. Tracy does not define what "more" is but she continues to process what this means for her at this juncture in her life. Accepting her singleness does not mean that she is happy or satisfied with her choice all of the time. "The issue of defining authenticity is a life theme that continues to recycle and what makes this issue more poignant in midlife, however, is that we are programmed to believe that we should have "already have gotten there" by then."[22]

DEFINING AN AUTHENTIC LIFE AS AN AGING ADULT

Defining an authentic life also carries over into other areas of concern. For SAACW growing older is a difficult emotional task where many questions are raised about mortality, relationships, health, fitness, finances and retirement. The future for midlife single women may not include persons to care for them if they have not established familial and friendship support networks. This is a major concern for women who are growing older and the necessity of having friends, family and financial support to help sustain them throughout life.

In addition to care-giving concerns, there are physical, as well as mental needs that are amplified during this transitional phase. Even more, questions about financial stability surface during this poignant progression in life. All of these factors lead to deeper questions about the vitality and mortality of their lives. There are the deeper philosophical and spiritual

22. Ibid.

questions about death, the soul and what is left behind after transition. In their *Narratives of Midlife and Growing Older* Diane, Angie and Tracy explore their apprehensions about growing older.

Narratives of Midlife and Growing Older

Diane, age 43: My concern is losing my mom. Both of my parents are alive, but losing my mom and not having no one else that I know truly loves me unconditionally in my life concerns me. I know that you can't say how you are going to go because my mom could outlive me. But my mom is thirty years older than me and I worry about what my life would be like without her. Being that I don't have a husband or children and I lose my mother, I wonder if the relationships that I've formed and created as family will be enough to sustain me as I grow older. I question if I will be one of those people who as I grow older will continue meeting people and doing things, always making friends and relationships.

Angie, age 48: Well, I think my health is a major concern. I've started to embrace a healthier lifestyle and eat healthier. I'm trying to incorporate more exercise and self care, especially being as busy as I am. Right now I'm focused on losing this weight and I'm doing it for health reasons not vanity—trying to catch somebody, I'm doing it for my health. Now that I'm older, I want to be financially set for retirement. From working with seniors and seeing so many of them struggling because of health, I want to make sure I'm financially healthy. I have a financial planner—I started budgeting and I'm careful about what I spend my money on. I got this student loan from seminary hanging over my head, I'm just preparing for it and I will deal with it as it comes.

Tracy, age 53: Financial security—I think often about what's going to happen as I grow older with being alone and needing care even though I'm healthy and doing well—I'm not sick, but I think about that. I worry about leaving a legacy and having someone to leave a legacy to. I don't want to leave this place and people not know who I am or recognize the contribution that I've made and acknowledge that it is worth something. Obviously when you are married with children there is a natural attention to who you are, your value and your worth.

Maintaining and deepening friendships is an important resource for single women in midlife transition.[23] "For the single childless person, friends are family and they are a great resource in times of stress."[24] Friends provide feedback, honesty, encouragement, and challenge. "Research shows that people with strong friendships experience less stress, recover more quickly from heart attacks and are likely to live longer than the friendless."[25] Moreover, women have a greater tendency than men do to "tend and be-friend" when under stress. Growing older without the support of a husband or children and having to rely on other forms of support via friendships or extended family members is life changing in some cases. The fear of not having adequate support systems in place or the fear of growing older alone is a sobering reality for midlife single women.

Diane fears growing older because she doesn't want to go through the pain of losing her mom and the support that has sustained and nourished her for much of her life. She wonders if the established friendships that she has acquired over the years will be enough to support her later in life. More importantly, will her support systems sustain, love and extend care "unconditionally" like her mother. Diane questions whether or not she will acquire new friends as she grows older. The value of maintaining and deepening friendships are as follows: "you have a shared history; you don't have to introduce yourself; friends remember how you were when you were younger."[26] Friendships offer other benefits for women without husbands and children. "Friendships are voluntary and they offer a way of inventing and re-inventing oneself in an authentic way throughout life."[27] Overall, friendships are a great asset to midlife single women in times of stress and critical life events. They provide a strong support network of alliances that provide many benefits in the long run.

Tracy has similar concerns about *connecting with future generations* in terms of the legacy that she has developed.[28] "An important aspect of this is being able to experience oneself as part of an ongoing historical flow and for the person without children; this historical linkage will need to

23. Ibid., 94.

24. Ibid.

25. Duenwald, "Some Friends," line 1.

26. Ibid.

27. O'Connor, "Women's Friendships," 118.

28. Ibid., 92.

be created."[29] Tracy now has the opportunity to discover new paths as she thinks about the legacy that is important to her. As she states, "I worry about leaving a legacy and having someone to leave a legacy to." Several suggestions are noted for connecting with future generations: "getting in touch with mentors in the past and directly expressing one's appreciation, leaving tangible work by actively mentoring younger people in or outside one's field, deepening relationships of diverse ethnic groups and populations, or modifying closely developed relationships."[30] Tracy has reached a period in life where she is very reflective and sensitive about her "worth and contributions" that will potentially reach another generation given the fact that she doesn't have a husband or children to carry on her legacy. Connecting with her nieces, nephews, cousins and extended family members are ways to bridge the gap with future generations in her family of origin.

In addition to maintaining and deepening friendships, connecting with future generations, *health, fitness* and *finances* are essential to the livelihood of SAACW. With the increasing demands of work, family, church and personal life, there are many health risks for African American women. With the prevalence of heart disease, breast cancer, diabetes, HIV/AIDS and mental health issues to name a few, the life expectancy of African American women is far less than their White female counterparts.[31] "Life expectancy is not only about how long African American women are expected to live, but it is also a good indication of how they are meeting the enormous challenges of society, as compared to other women."[32] Race, gender, economics, social, familial, religious and sexual biases are also harmful stressors in the lives of African American women. Emile M. Townes, in *Breaking the Fine Rain of Death: African American Health Issues of a Womanist Ethic of Care*, shares the "communal lament in Black America:

1. Black women live fewer years than White women,

2. our breast cancer is caught later, and we are more likely to die of it,

3. the majority of women and children infected with HIV disease are Black,

4. our children are more likely to be born small, and they die more frequently before reaching one year of age,

29. Ibid.
30. Ibid., 92–93.
31. Fisher Collins, "Commentary on the Health," 1.
32. Ibid.

5. we have heart disease at younger ages; a heart attack is more likely to prove fatal; and we have twice as many cases of high blood pressure as Whites,

6. nearly 50 percent of us are overweight,

7. we are more likely to smoke, and we are less likely to quit than White woman,

8. we have higher rates of sexually transmitted infection and pelvic inflammatory disease, and

9. over half of us have been beaten, been raped, or survived incest."[33]

Therefore, the increasing health risks that are prevalent for African American women are even more challenging for aging African American women who may or may not be as assertive in managing their health, fitness and mental well-being. Angie and Tracy share their concerns in this area.

Angie is managing a "healthier lifestyle" through diet and exercise because she knows the risks of inadequate "self-care." How well she manages her emotional, spiritual, psychological and physical health will have some ramifications later in life. Tracy acknowledges that the longevity of her life is dependent upon not "getting sick" because she worries about who will take care of her. As stated above, there are enormous challenges that are biological, social, environmental, and economic that has a profound impact on the health and well-being of SAACW.

As well, taking the necessary steps to secure ones financial health and stability is crucial in midlife. Saving for retirement and making sure that there are enough provisions for health care cost, housing needs, and preparing end of life wishes are all necessary steps for planning the future. Angie and Tracy are concerned about their financial stability and how it will impact them later in life. Angie is more proactive in the ways the she has planned for her financial future and has taken the necessary steps to set parameters on how she manages her finances. Second, strategically planning for the repayment of her student loan is critical for her financial future. Tracy, on the other hand is concerned about "financial security" and how it directly impacts her health care needs. She does not state how she plans on implementing the necessary changes for securing her financial future but reflecting on these possible financial outcomes is challenging for her.

---

33. Townes, *Breaking the Fine Rain of Death*, 120.

SUMMARY

In summary, midlife is a phase of "alternative scripts" and critical reflection.[34] Being single in midlife doesn't abort a woman's strength, vitality or personhood. Several midlife transitions were addressed in this chapter: the ideal family, motherhood, authenticity, work, and growing older. These discussions lead to other understandings about loneliness, aloneness, regret, intimacy and fear. By and large, midlife represents a coming into one's own purpose, discerning what matters most, discovering a deeper sense of the self, and facing fears that come with growing older.

34. Ibid.

Chapter 4

"There Is No Such Thing as the Ideal Marriage or Family"

WHO OR WHAT IS THE "IDEAL" FAMILY FOR SAACW IN MIDLIFE?

There is a certain mythology that encompasses marriage and family. Marriage is often romanticized as the ultimate end goal of a person's life. The image of the wife, husband, children with a home and white picket fence is ideally the image that has been circulated in popular culture. The model ideal family has been the nuclear family which is comprised of the breadwinner father, domestic mother and children. These images of marriage and family are like well-oiled tapes that are played constantly in social outlets and are the foundational structure of our society. However, the typical breadwinning father and domesticated mother prototype does not lend itself to a broader world view that honors singleness and other varied forms of family in the society.

Marriage is considered the hallmark of American society. The build up to the wedding means securing the right partner and purchasing the perfect wedding gown. Not far in the background are romantic notions about "falling in love" that have been circulated in folktales, myths and legends. Prince Charming is a male character that rescues the damsel in distress and they ride together in the sunset happily ever after. The symbolism is that the Prince Charming sweeps away the damsel from all of her troubles and problems. Other contemporary analogies include finding the perfect soul mate. The soul mate is the person that "gets you," was meant to be with you, and is able to connect on a deep and intimate level. This person is expected to solve all problems, meet specific needs and personal fulfillment in one's life. Therefore, this chapter examines how marriage and family have informed societal norms of today. The *Narratives of the Ideal Family, Ideal Marriage* and *Ideal Marriage and the Black Church* take into consideration the mythology of the ideal from the lens of SAACW.

THE "IDEAL" FAMILY

The traditional ideal family is understood as the nuclear family; father, mother and children in marriage. "In the United States the two eras have been mythologized: the traditional family of the preindustrial past and the nuclear family of the 1950s."[1] The burgeoning image of the ideal family of the 1950s placed an emphasis on finding happiness within the nuclear family. Because these images were endorsed in the wider culture, single people and people of color often found themselves displaced during this time. Froma Walsh, in *Normal Family Processes, Growing Diversity and Complexity*, describes those cherished nostalgic families of the past:

> From the generation of the "baby boomers," TV dramas such as *Little House on the Prairie* transported viewers back to the distant rural past, to a time of large stable families, homespun values, and multigenerational connectedness. Family series such as *Ozzie and Harriet* and *Leave It to Beaver*, idealized the mid-20th century white middle class, suburban nuclear family, headed by the breadwinner father and supported by the homemaker mother. The lasting popularity of such images expressed longing for not only a romanticized notion of the family but also seemingly simpler, happier, and more secure times. Over recent decades, family sitcoms have gradually portrayed a broader spectrum of family life amid striking social change. Family sitcoms such as *Modern Family* offer less idealized images and more varied complex patterns in the "new normal" family life.[2]

The 1950s era represented many marital perceptions and understandings. During this time people were very invested in their courtships and

---

1. Walsh, "New Normal Diversity," 9.
2. Ibid.

the mores of the ideal family. Stephanie Coontz, in *Marriage, A History: How Love Conquered Marriage*, further describes the ethos surrounding marriage in the era of *Ozzie and Harriet* and *Leave It to Beaver*.

> Never before has so many people shared the experience of court-ing their own mates, getting married at will, and setting up their own household. Never had married couples been so independent of extended family and community groups. And never had so many people agreed that only one kind of family was "normal." . . . Even people who had grown up in completely different family systems had come to believe that universal marriage at a young age into a male breadwinner family was the traditional and permanent form of marriage.[3]

Coontz purports that everyone patterned the ideal family with the bread-winner husband and homemaker wife. In the United States marriage was seen as the only suitable path for the single young adult. A 1957 survey taken in the United States reported that four out of five people believed that anyone who preferred to remain single was, "sick," "neurotic," or "immoral."[4] Furthermore, women who did not conform to the ideal home-maker image were viewed as persons with serious psychological problems.[5] The ideal television families were revered to a great extent because families wanted to ensure that they looked the part of the happy family relation-ally and materially. Iconic shows such as *Ozzie and Harriet* and *Leave It to Beaver* set the bar for family consumerism of many home appliances that appealed to the families of this time. Again, this concept equated happiness with the purchase of such home appliances.[6]

In contrast, the concept of the ideal family for Black families was repre-sented in popular television shows of the 1970s and 1980s such as *Good Times*, *The Jeffersons*, and *The Cosby Show*. *Good Times* showcased the impoverished African American family who lived in the Chicago housing project with the breadwinner father James Evans and the homemaker wife Florida Evans along with their three children, James Jr. (JJ), Thelma and Michael. Despite the scarcity and limited resources available, the Evans family enjoyed "good times in the midst of their struggle." *The Jeffersons*, however, showcased an af-fluent African American couple, George and Louise Jefferson, and their only

3. Coontz, *Marriage*, 229.
4. Ibid., 230.
5. Ibid.
6. Ibid., 232.

child, Lionel. George was a successful breadwinner husband who owned a dry cleaning business. *The Cosby Show* depicted the upper-middle-class African American family with two successful parents, an obstetrician husband, Cliff Huxtable, and attorney wife, Clair Huxtable. This power couple had five children, Sondra, Denise, Theodore (Theo), Vanessa, and Rudy. *The Cosby Show* contrasted its understanding of the negative images of African American families and traditional gender roles by introducing a broader audience to a positive, supportive upper-middle-class African American family and "changed the direction of Black representation in the media" with traditional family values.[7] However, some believe that it also portrayed similar nostalgic attitudes that were depicted in the White middle-class families of the past and "misdirected many of the socioeconomic issues" endemic to African American communities.[8] To date, some African American families resonate with the social consciousness raised in all of these African American televisions programs while others do not. Nevertheless, marriages and families of today are impacted by a multiplicity of factors such as race, ethnicity, gender, religion, and socioeconomic issues that are compounded by complex family systems in social context.

Thus, the image of the ideal family as illustrated in the iconic television programs of the 1950s, 60s, 70s, and 80s are images that the participants watched during their formative years. Families and marriages of today are less romantic and multifaceted than what has been portrayed on television. The concept of the ideal family is explored in what I am calling the *Narratives of the Ideal Family*.

Narratives of the Ideal Family

> Diane, age 43: I don't think any family or marriage is ideal but it's what you make it. When you become an adult and you live your life and time passes, you can say who is in your family and who's not, even if they are not blood related to you. So church family are my family, friends that I've grown up with, new friends that I've met and share a part of my life, to me that is what family is. It doesn't have to look like the nuclear family because that doesn't mean family. Some people have that and it's not good.

7. Gates and Higginbotham, *African American Lives*, 195.
8. Ibid.

Angie, age 48: I think there is no such thing as the ideal family. I think society has crafted the nuclear family as the ideal family, but that's not attainable for everyone. Hopefully the family you have is the family that's loving and supportive. As long as you have that support mechanism that's primary then that is your family. I would say my immediate family and that would be my mother and sister.

Tracy, age 53: I think there is a cultural norm established. The traditional concept is not what is use to be, we are blended families and the like. As a single woman, family extends beyond my biological family. I consider my friends as family. The people I spend the greater amount of time with are family to me. For me family is the familiar that care and love me intimately without conditions. And for me those are my friends. Their expectations are low and their acceptance is high—we are who we are. They are family to me and we work through difficulties as would any family. The ideal family I don't know, you would first have to define ideal. Ideal would be relative to the person that has to make that decision. Ideal for me would not be ideal for the next person. As a child June Cleaver was the ideal mom, I didn't see moms like that but that's what I aspired to. I was a *Leave It to Beaver* fan, I couldn't wait until it came on, I liked *I Love Lucy*, Lucy was funny, she was free, she dressed up, looked pretty and just enjoyed life, she was crazy, but it was okay because she had a man that loved her, family, friends. African American's women's experiences were not like that. And I never saw that until later in life when I began to see them in Florida Evans in *Good Times*. We saw Florida Evan struggling that was the reality and not something to be idealized because who wanted to be the mom that was always complaining, struggling, and crying, "Lord help me" who wants that.

The ideal family is not as ideal and static like it has been in the past. Family, as described in this narrative, is defined as those groups of persons who provide substantial support. Family is comprised of blood-related kin and non-blood-related kin. Diane's family support is comprised of non-blood-related family such as church members, long-term friendships and new friendships that she has developed. The quality and longevity of her friendships is what determines the family bond. Angie has a strong support from her mother and sister; however, she recognizes that regardless of the blood ties, family is the "loving" and "supportive mechanism" for each person. Tracy's friends more so than her blood-related kin are her family. She describes several characteristics that her friends exemplify. They are individuals who are willing to invest their time, resources and unconditional support. Families of the twenty-first century are more blended and extended than ideal.

Tracy recalls many of the idyllic television programs that shaped her understanding of marriage and family. There is a notable difference in how she perceived the White female homemakers June Cleaver and Lucy Ricardo versus the Black female homemaker Florida Evans. The attitudes and characteristics of June Cleaver and Lucy Ricardo were perceived as "happy" while the attitudes and characteristics of Florida Evans were perceived as "unhappy." Tracy was very clear in the image that served her best as she stated, no one wanted to be the "Lord help me," struggling mom like Florida Evans. According to Tracy, Florida Evans mirrored the sobering realities within the African American community more than the nostalgic family values as typified in White American society. Similarly, Lucy Ricardo looked the part of the happy "pretty" wife. Despite her antics, Tracy viewed her as a woman who had all that she needed in life, the "love and support of her husband, family and friends." As a young girl, Tracy idealized the perfect family and perfect wives that were circulated in mainstream television media.

Overall, family, as described by Diane, Angie and Tracy are those relationships that provide bonds of support and that have been cultivated over the years. Family is understood as blood related, friendships and communal support. Tracy sums up her friendship family as one who "works through difficulties." This is her realistic family versus the idyllic images that she remembers on television. The imagery of the ideal family is one that is whole, normal and problem-free.[9] However, in reality adhering to the ideal image does not necessarily mean that families experience wholeness in the context that is perfect or ideal. As Diane names, "some people have families, but it's not good."

THE "IDEAL" MARRIAGE AND VICTORIAN BELIEFS

Many embedded beliefs about marriage and family are predicated on another illusionary image of "romantic love" that was introduced in the Victorian era. The Victorians imposed a set of values and beliefs about marriage, love and intimacy that conformed how people thought and lived. During this time, people were known for their strict morality and respectability in life. Marriage, family, home, church and society were grounded on these

9. Ibid., 5.

puritanical belief systems that dominated the nineteenth century. The Victorians advocated for couples to "fall in love" and that marriage was based on this principle. Stephanie Coontz, in *Marriage, A History: How Love Conquered Marriage*, describes the mannerisms of the Victorians during this era. "They were the first people in history to try and make marriage the pivotal experience in people's lives and married love the principal focus of their emotions, obligations, and satisfactions."[10] Victorian marriages were invested in beliefs about "romantic love, intimacy, personal fulfillment, and mutual happiness."[11] However, their beliefs also collided with their rigid views about sex and gender roles. Coontz purports:

> The people who took up idealization of love and intimacy to new heights during the Nineteenth century did not intend to shake up marriage or unleash a new preoccupation with sexual gratification. They meant to strengthen marriage by encouraging husbands and wives to weave emotional bonds. In the long run they weakened it. The focus on romantic love eventually undercut the doctrine of separate spheres for men and women and the ideal of female purity, putting new strains on the institution of marriage.[12]

The ideology of separate spheres relegated men and women to specific roles and spheres within the society.[13] Men were assigned to the public sphere of business, commerce and politics, while women were relegated to the private sphere of the home and family.[14] Men were viewed as more intellectual while women were regulated by their sexuality and reproductive systems.[15] These dichotomies carried over in other understandings about female purity and chastity. The ideal woman was "virtuous, pious and respectable, the kind of woman a man would want to marry and the kind of woman a good girl would wish to be."[16] Women were asexual beings who were expected to keep themselves "pure" and remain virgins until marriage. If a woman did have sexual relations with a man she was considered a "fallen woman." Sex was not something that the Victorians talked about openly; public discourse on this topic was considered a social taboo. However, it

10. Ibid., 177.

11. Ibid.

12. Ibid., 178.

13. Gordon and Nair, *Public Lives*, 1.

14. Ibid.

15. Ibid., 2.

16. Ibid., 159.

was not a social taboo for men to have as many sexual partners as they liked. They did not have to remain chaste like their female counterparts.

Thus, the realities of the Victorian era were filled with many contradictions in their pursuit of love and happiness. "The rigid separation between men's and women's spheres made it hard for couples to share their innermost dreams, no matter how much in love they were—the ideal of intimacy was continually undermined in practice by the reality of the different constraints on men and women, leading to a "sense of estrangement" between many husbands and wives."[17] The distinctions outlined in the separate spheres indicate the disadvantages that women faced as they were legally given over to their husbands. On the surface marriage appeared romantic, but the actual institution benefited men more so than women. Women did not have rights within marriage or outside of it.[18] If they had any concerns wisely they "kept their aspirations in check and swallowed their disappointments."[19] Largely, marriage was seen as a means to an end. Without the confines of marriage, women had no other means of income. For all intense purposes they were dependent upon the financial support of men because of the social stratifications in mainstream Victorian society. Coontz gives a full description of how single women faired in the Victorian period:

> Single women could rarely support themselves living on their own for more than a few years at a time, much less save for their old age. Many women saw marriage as the only alternative to destitution or prostitution or, even in the best case, genteel dependence on relatives. In absence of job security and pensions, a woman who was not married by her thirties generally had to move in with relatives. Sentimental novels aside, this was not always an idyllic life.[20]

Single women were forced to fend for themselves during the Victorian era. However, the realities of single women are very different today. Single women are gainfully employed and have planned for their financial future. They are not so dependent on their families for financial and other means of support. However, there are certain single women and midlife single women who are dependent on their families for support because of illness, financial calamity or divorce. Diane, Angie and Tracy's *Narratives of the Ideal Marriage* explore the concept of marriage and how this iconic institution is viewed from their familial and societal expectations.

17. Ibid., 188.
18. Ibid., 187.
19. Ibid., 185.
20. Ibid.

Narratives of the Ideal Marriage

Diane, age 43: I wouldn't mind being married but if I don't get married I'm okay. The scary part I see now is my mother forsaking herself because my father is very ill. Even the doctors say we don't know how this man is still alive. Her whole life is taking care of him. We have a joke in our family, they have been married 49 years but the joke my mother says is, "I've been married for 49 years and he's been married seven years. He's been ill and can't take care of himself, doesn't know his butt from his elbow. My mother has been diligently taking care of him for the last seven years. We all know that if things were different, we wouldn't see him half the time. That's just my father; he started being home when he got sick. My father had lots of affairs. He's lived with other women still married to my mom. He has other children, but I don't think we will find out until he passes away. I understand why my mom did it. My mother was a teenage mother and she had a daughter and that relationship didn't work and when she met my dad, she got married. She was staying married; she wasn't going to have two kids by two different men and be unmarried. So it didn't matter what my father did, she didn't want to face the world as a single women with two different kids by different fathers. If that's what it is going take to be married, then I can't deal with it. I really want it to be joyful and meshing.

Angie, age 48: I think marriage is great for those seeking to be married. I am ecstatic for people who are able to find happiness in marriage and do so without pressure, manipulation or coercion. At this point I don't have a desire to be married and that could change but I just enjoy wearing my white robe to marry people as opposed to just looking for the white dress to be in a wedding. So I got excited when I got my first white robe to marry someone. I don't get that same kind of feeling when I look at wedding books and that kind of thing, I've never done that.

Tracy, age 53: Yes, I think marriage is a beautiful thing. I think family is important or we cease to exist. Marriage and family are more important than our current society gives credit to. I am open to marriage although I'm not as hopeful about a family for obvious reasons; I'm 53 so I don't think I will be birthing any babies anytime soon. And I have observed enough to know that it is not a task that is easy to undertake and I don't even know that I could raise a child in this society right now.

Diane, Angie and Tracy view marriage from diverse contextual lenses. Diane would like to marry one day; however, she is fearful of the infidelity and the family dynamics that shaped her parents' marriage. Much like the separate spheres in the Victorian era, her father's indiscretions were not hidden from the family. In order to process what transpired between her parents, Diane connects with her mother's narrative. As a young teenager, Diane's mother had a baby out of wedlock and felt strongly that marriage would fix her dilemma. First, marriage would right the wrong and shame of having a child out of wedlock. Second, staying in an estranged marriage was better than facing the world as a single Black mother and as a perceived "fallen" woman in the society. Diane views marriage as a state of forsaking oneself, after all this is what her mother modeled in taking care of her sick husband and staying in a less than ideal marriage. Diane's fear is that she doesn't want to forsake her happiness or sacrifice herself at the expense of a divisive marriage.

Angie, on the other hand, does not feel the urge to marry at this time in her life. Although she is supportive of those who wish to marry, marriage is not something that she desires. Angie pulls away from the stereotypical wedding fanfare and "wedding dress" image that is immersed in the culture. The cultural milieu suggests that every young girl dreams about marrying the perfect husband and envisions her wedding day and wedding gown. Angie, however, had different dreams and aspirations. As an ordained minister, she connects more with helping couples to establish their covenant in marriage. What is ideal about marriage is her freedom of choice. Angie decides whether or not marriage is the "ideal" path for her. Similarly, Tracy has some cultural beliefs about marriage and what is ideal in regards to family. Marriage means the existence, survival and continuation of the family. However, Tracy feels some trepidation over raising a child in this current society.

Diane, Angie and Tracy's perceptions of marriage were informed by their family histories, societal myths and beliefs. These are real considerations that would impact a person's decision to marry. The analogy of "white" as denoted in Angie's narrative stereotypically represents the innocence, purity and wholeness that symbolize marriage. In real life, the wedding in all of the trimmings is one consideration; however, the "meshing" of two lives and "raising a child" is a serious undertaking that is often overlooked in the excitement of the wedding day.

THE "IDEAL" MARRIAGE AND THE BLACK CHURCH

Religion plays an important role in the lives of many African American women as they represent a large percentage of the churches membership including men two to one.[21] With the pervasive understanding of Victorian and idyllic beliefs that have shaped Western culture, the Black church is not immune to similar beliefs about love and marriage. Romantic love and the urgency of finding a partner is a strong message within the Black church. Deborrah Cooper, in "Does the Black Church Keep Black Women Single?" claims that "African American women want men to which they are equally yoked (2 Cor 6:14)—a man that goes to church five times a week and every Sunday just like they do."[22] The implication here is that women who are equally yoked will find personal fulfillment, satisfaction and happiness with mates who have similar ideologies about God, church, and worship.[23] However, the underlying message is that relationships that are not grounded in similar ideologies, strong Christian practices or sound values and beliefs are destined for failure. The ideal marriage and relationship is one that is saturated with God, Bible and the church. Somehow, marriage "in the church" legitimates the longevity of the union and marriage between Christian persons legitimates similar marital values and beliefs. In fact, the "divorce rates among born again Christians (this rate includes church denomination groups) is 32 percent, which is identical to the 33 percent figure among non born again adult groups."[24]

Another caveat is that African American men much like all men of diverse ethnic groups are not regular attendees in Sunday morning worship services. According to the PEW study, "African American men are significantly more likely than women to be unaffiliated with any religion (16 vs. 9 percent); nearly one-in-five men say they have no formal religious affiliation."[25] Finding a suitable partner for life is the mandate of many churches including the Black church. A favorite and beloved Scripture that is quoted in the Black church is, "He who finds a wife, finds a good thing and receives favor from the Lord" (Prov 18:22). The implication in this passage is that God glorifies marriage and the role of a wife as something

21. Snorton, "Angry Black Women," 213.
22. Ibid., line 17.
23. *Essence*, "What It Means to Be 'Equally Yoked.'"
24. Barrick, "Christian Divorce Rate," line 33.
25. Saghal and Smith, "Religious Portrait of African Americans," line 36.

pleasing, religious, good and divinely inspired. Many single African American women may feel out of place or unfavored by God because they have not fulfilled the role of a wife as mandated by the Bible and God. The interpretation of "good" brings about many assumptions and questions about whether or not single Christian women are "good" in and of themselves or if they are "good" and acceptable in the context of marriage. Understandably, the contextual lens of the Judaic community places women in esteemed roles of wife and mother. However, the problem is that the Black church continues to relegate African American women to these traditional biblical roles in the twenty-first century, sometimes refusing to see them in other roles that are befitting of the changing times and culture. The husband "finds" the wife; however, the passage doesn't suggest how he should find his wife or if he should find a wife in the church. Therefore, is it practical for single African American women to take matters into their own hands to "find" husbands or is this antithetical to the Bible and teachings of the Black church? These are the present realities of the SAACW as they discuss their perspectives in their *Narratives of Marriage and the Black Church.*

Narratives of Marriage and the Black Church

Diane, age 43: You are not complete. Like whatever is wrong with you we are going to pray that thing away, so you can find a husband. You should be actively finding a husband so what's wrong with you? Time is running out. You are cute now but you are not always going to be cute. Really, I think I get better looking as I get older.

Angie, age 48: Church mimics society, you have to marry. As a single woman you are expected to find a husband and even if you excel professionally or educationally you still are seen as a failure if you don't get husband or child. A lot of this, especially if you don't have children, is rooted in biblically imagery because the barren woman is seen as a woman without purpose, so bareness is a sin really. The church carries a lot of that today.

Tracy, age 53: Just find it. There is no class no direction just meet a man—date and all of that, but there is no direction. Of course everyone wants you to marry a minister or deacon and try to put you with every single man that comes through the door, but there is no direction, I'll figure it out on my own, still trying to figure that out.

The Black church and religion on a large scale has certain attitudes about marriage and family as denoted in these narratives. Marriage epitomizes a woman's worth and attractiveness in the culture, church and society. An unmarried older woman is an unattractive woman in a youth driven culture. The older single woman who cannot fulfill the role of wife or mother are placed in the "wifely," "motherly" role in which they are responsible for the needs of the church body.

Subsequently, the Black church upholds biblical beliefs about a woman's ability to procreate and "to be fruitful and multiply" (Gen 1:28) from a hermeneutical lens of marriage, family and creation. However, the implication is that regardless of how well African American women "excel" in their personal and professional lives, the traditional roles of wife and mother are primary. Jana Marguerite Bennett, in *Water Is Thicker than Blood: An Augustinian Theology of Marriage and Singleness*, elaborates on the use of the Genesis texts for theologically understanding marriage and family. She asserts that the "Genesis texts necessitates grappling with male and female gender roles (Adam as lord over Eve) and issues about procreation (the injunction to "be fruitful and multiply") whereby gender, sex and gendered roles become central issues."[26]

Another central issue that is significant to gender roles is barrenness. Barrenness is considered a social taboo in the culture, church and society because it relegates women to their reproductive bodies. The countless barren women in the Bible who were barren temporarily or permanently all have different stories and experiences; however, their barrenness and the inability to produce a male child was a blemish in the scrutinizing eyes of their communities and within their own psyches as women. First Timothy 2:15 states, ". . . yet she will be saved through childbearing provided they continue in faith and love and holiness with modesty." Where this places women who are unable to conceive and how salvation is connected to their reproductive capability is challenging. Does this passage signify that single childless women are not saved? Furthermore, does this indicate that single childless women are not included in the household of God? Families are uplifted and are a central focus in the Bible and the Black church; however, this passage places single women on the periphery of what constitutes family in the Black church setting. Bennett denotes that "the picture of Christian households is incomplete if we do not consider singleness, partly because considering singleness is recognition that households do not bear identical character to

26. Bennett, *Water Is Thicker*, 55.

each other, the baptized are not all married with children, nor does it appear that marriage and family should be the main emphasis for Christians."[27]

These and other similar views impact single Christian women today. The understanding is that single women are expected to wait in a church container for their husbands because their husbands will find them. Some Black churches take a very literal interpretation of the Bible and believe that dating is antithetical to Scripture. After all, where do you find examples of dating in the Bible? Tracy explains that "there is no class or direction," the overall message from the Black church is "just meet a man." Meeting and dating a man is a temporary fix for singleness, however, marriage is considered the end goal. Moreover, if a single woman wants to be held in high esteem then she should marry a "pastor," "deacon" or "minister." The Black church and churches overall are inundated with many embedded beliefs about marriage and family. Angie explains that the Black church mirrors the society in what is good, proper and respectable for women and certainly marriage and family.

EXTENDED AND FICTIVE FAMILY KINSHIP IN AN AFRICAN AMERICAN CONTEXT

The question therefore is what constitutes family for SAACW? Because SAACW do not have husbands or sometimes children like their married counterparts, family takes on diverse meanings. This discourse examines the ideal family from a nuclear family position that has been established through mainstream iconic television programs of the 1950s, 60s, 70s and 80s. However, family encompasses established networks or relationships that may include blood-related family as well as non-blood-related family. During times of transition, family and community support is essential. In many cases, SAACW find other means of support when they have deviated from family expectations. Or they may have support from their blood-related families, but also expanded support from those of their extended and fictive families.

The term extended family has been applied to a kinship network or as people who are "grafted into families and they are a functioning part of the group."[28] In an African American context, extended family means mother, father, brother, sister, cousin, aunt, uncle, and endearing terms such as play mother, play father, play sister, play brother, church family, church minister

27. Ibid., 83.

28. Belgave and Allison, *African American Psychology*, 153.

or church pastor.[29] The extended family is an important network that provides emotional, economic and spiritual support. People of African descent survived the perils of slavery, racism and oppression because of the support from extended family. Carroll A. Watkins Ali, in *Survival and Liberation: Pastoral Theology in African American Context*, explains the role of the extended family and the "collective support, resistance, and resilience of the slave community."[30]

> Although Africans were forced to let go of their language and many of their rituals, they held firmly to the African philosophy of life expressed in the African proverb: I am because we are and because we are, therefore I am. Thus, sticking together and taking care of one another proved to be a real strength of resistance. Networks of extended family and kinships continued to nurture and care for children who were orphaned by death and separation from parents on the auction block, offsetting the intended destruction familial unity among slaves.[31]

The extended kinship family still holds true today for African American people. The traditions that have systemically provided the collective support of African American families also provide similar support for single African American women who rely on the Black church for spiritual direction and emotional well being. Therefore, the Black church has served as an extended family because it has provided the collective support for diverse families in peril. The implication of the extended family including the Black church is its emphasis on "those relationships that share blood and are metaphorically linked through their shared pain, history, goals, experiences, interest and hope of liberation."[32]

It is important to note that the Black church has been the center of the Black family, yet it has faced some challenges within a changing society. The ideal family mythology as examined in this discourse also applies to the Black church. It is not a perfect institution. With that being said, some individuals experience it as a place of liberation and oppression. African American women like so many women of diverse ethnic groups support their churches but are not equally regarded in leadership roles and opportunities in some cases. Therefore, it can be said that the Black church is

---

29. Boyd-Franklin, *Black Families in Therapy*, 59.
30. Watkins Ali, *Survival and Liberation*, 19.
31. Ibid.
32. Smith, *The Church in the Life*, 41.

life giving in some instances and a hindrance in other instances. The point here is to explore the ways in which the Black church in its inception has sustained many individuals for the most part in their casualties of life and is an extended resource for families, women, men, youth and children.

In the same way that the extended family involves the shared experiences between a collective group both within and without the Black church; fictive kinship involves a shared interest between members. Fictive kinship is defined as those kinship relationships that are not necessarily defined by biology and marriage alone, yet they are important and are sometimes more important than those relationships that are created biologically and through marriage.[33] Much like the extended family, these relationships include godparents, play moms and dads, girlfriends, guy friends, adoptive friends, sorority sisters and work friends. There are fictive friendships in which SAACW befriend other single women and single men. As Tracy explained, "single friends can pick up and go spontaneously because there is no little league practice or ballet rehearsal to worry about on Saturday." Spending time with friends does break the monotony particularly when you share special interest and activities. Tracy's inner circle of single friends "keep it real" and they challenge one another when necessary. They also celebrate birthdays, accomplishments and travel together. Her fictive single friends help her when she has medical emergencies and are a source of support during illness. Diane has similar fictive friendships that support her when she needs assistance. "Fictive relationships serve to broaden mutual support networks, create a sense of community, enhance social control and regularize interactions with people otherwise outside the boundaries of family."[34]

Single African American women seek communities in which to care and to be cared for in their life's journey. The concerns of SAACW as it pertains to life, death, growing older, work, finances, health and adoption alongside shedding some of the romantic illusions of marriage and partnership raise questions about what constitutes family and care. Diane and Tracy, in the *Narratives of Family*, define family from extended and fictive communities of care. Girlfriends and church family are the means in which they have established family in addition to their biological bonds. This is not to say that other single ethnic groups don't experience extended bonds in the same way, but it suggests that extended family and fictive kin have

33. Wagner, "Fictive Kinship," line 1.
34. Ibid., line 15.

been a major source of strength for many African American families and single African American women within the African American context.

Nancy Boyd Franklin, in *Black Families In Therapy: Understanding the African American Experience*, elaborates on *reciprocity* from Carol Stack's anthropological research in the extended family network. Reciprocity, as defined by Carol Stack, is "the process of helping each other and exchanging support as well as goods and services."[35] SAACW negotiate their basic necessities in life such as car maintenance, home repairs, and other services with extended and fictive family.

"Reciprocity takes on many forms from lending money to taking out 'kin insurance' by taking care of a relative's child with the understanding that similar help will be returned when needed."[36] For SAACW who desire children, reciprocity and childcare works in establishing a legacy with children for mentorship and future connections. Furthermore, extended care networks also take the form of emotional support, knowing that the extended family can be counted on to "share the burden" in times of trouble, and that one will offer emotional support in return.[37] Establishing family is a work in progress and Stakes cautions against reciprocity and the danger of exhausting oneself in the process of support.[38] The implication is that extended and fictive families operate in mutual ways that are supportive for all parties involved.

FINAL POINTS

Finally, the concept of ideal and the perfect state of marriage, family, extended family, fictive family and singleness does not exist. "Philip Culbertson in *Caring For God's People* sums up the descriptions of families that is much wider than the public media suggest, families of today consist of: married couples with young children; married couples who can't have children; married couples who choose not to have children; married couples with one parent in residence; solo parents with a child or children living with them, single parents whose children live elsewhere; stepfamilies and blended families and divorced couples who share custody of children; grandparents raising their grandchildren; adult brother and/or sisters living

35. Stack, *All of Our Kin*, 3.
36. Ibid., 54.
37. Ibid.
38. Ibid.

together; gay and lesbian couples without children; gay and lesbian couples with children."[39] I add to Culbertson's descriptions single people without biological children who share in the rearing of other children; single people who live on their own and have fictive friendships and extended families; romantic partners who cohabitate in various living arrangements, but may consider themselves single; common law couples with children; common law couples without children. Thus, families of today are flexible according to their diverse needs and functioning.

39. Culbertson, *Caring for God's People*, 12.

Chapter 5

"I Decided That I Can Do What I Want with My Body"

SAACW IN MIDLIFE: SEX, SEXUALITY AND SPIRITUALITY

There are many preconceived notions about sex and sexuality. Sexual expression is a healthy, natural and important aspect of life. Yet, how sex and sexuality are discussed and interpreted in contemporary culture shapes our attitudes and beliefs. One existing belief that is circulated in the Black church and other communal settings is the idea that our sexuality is something that should be ignored in the hopes that "it" will go away until the appropriate time. There is no middle ground. The solution to what is felt deep inside is to pretend that it simply doesn't exist. On the whole we are unsure how to discuss these private and intimate sexual feelings that all of creation experiences. Nonetheless, we feel ashamed over something that is a natural part of being human. The culture has its own value system in regards to sex and sexuality and so does the Black church. Nevertheless, all persons whether churched or un-churched cannot deny their own humanity and sexuality.

Therefore, this chapter wrestles with sex and sexuality from the perspectives of midlife women and how they have come to understand their own humanity, spirituality and sexuality. There are various sexual embedded beliefs that both liberate and oppress simultaneously. When we speak about sex and sexuality it is usually viewed from the vantage point of physical desires, longings, human anatomy and human expression. Yet, how does sex and sexuality connect with who we are as spiritual beings? The *Narratives of Sexuality and Spirituality, Virginity and Fornication, and Masturbation* examine sexuality and spirituality from a multiplicity of experiences and beliefs.

SEXUALITY AND SPIRITUALITY

What are some diverse perceptions and interpretations of sexuality and spirituality? Christian ethicist James B. Nelson, in *Embodiment: An Approach to Sexuality and Christian Theology*, states that "sexuality involves more than what we do with our genitals, it is who we are as body-selves who experience the emotional, cognitive, physical, and spiritual need for intimate communication—human and divine."[1] Womanist ethicist Emilie M. Townes, in *In a Blaze of Glory: Womanist Spirituality as Social Witness*, states, "Our sexuality is who we are as thinking, feeling, and caring human beings; it is our ability to love and nurture; to express warmth and compassion; it is not our gonads."[2] Townes speaks further about Alice Walker's four-part definition of *womanist* that encompass both individual and communal dimensions. "Black folk and Black women are sexual beings who are to be loved, sexually or not—the individual is grounded in love; love of self, love of community, love of the worlds of Black women, love of the Spirit."[3] A major dimension of sexuality and spirituality is the love of self which makes the love of others and God, sexually and spiritually possible.

Womanist theologian Kelly Brown Douglas, in *Sexuality and the Black Church: A Womanist Perspective*, denotes that "spirituality involves more than worship or prayer life or simply going to church, spirituality concerns a person's connection to God and thus, inevitably involves her or his sexuality."[4] Douglas elaborates on the connection of the White culture and its mark on Black Spirituality, human sexuality and the relationship to the divine:

> Human sexuality and Black spirituality is an appreciation of the embodied Black self that is loved and created in the image of God.

1. Nelson, *Embodiment*, 18.
2. Townes, *In a Blaze of Glory*, 81.
3. Ibid.
4. Brown-Douglas, *Sexuality and the Black Church*, 84.

> For Black people there is the contradiction between being created
> in the image of God and being made to feel that everything about
> who we are as Black people is inferior. To be able to love our own
> body is to be able to accept God's love of us. To be unable to love
> our bodies is not to know the full measure of God's love. It conse-
> quently means that we will not be able to share that love.[5]

"Both sexuality and spirituality reflect the human capacity—and embodied desire—for human connection."[6] Other correlations are as follows: "Both sexuality and spirituality signal the relational quality of being human—if human beings are called by God to be in relationship with God (our spirituality), then sexuality is a gift from God that helps make the relationship possible."[7]

All of these definitions and interpretations relate to various aspects that exist with being human, sexual and spiritual. Although a great polarity still exists in religious circles, it is important to examine where this dissension originates. Christianity borrowed many of its beliefs and perceptions about the physical, sexual and spiritual from Western thought as influenced by the Greco-Roman world.[8] These beliefs and perceptions were opposed to many of the qualities that make us human, including sexuality and spirituality. The early church forefathers borrowed many of their beliefs from Greco-Roman perceptions that devalued human sexuality as God's blessing to humanity. From this perspective, the human body and sexual pleasure, if not kept in check, have the propensity to separate humanity from their relations with God and Jesus Christ and if not careful, salvation.[9] The influence of the Greco-Roman worldview brought about a major perspective in how the body and sexual expression are devalued in Christianity today. Sexual expression is permitted only in instances of marriage and procreation; however, sexual expression outside of this mandate is denigrated. As stated earlier, sexuality and spirituality are relational to each other; however, the separation promotes an antagonistic view toward the relational aspects of sexuality and spirituality. These sentiments negate healthy discourse in the private, public and religious sector because it is viewed as promoting sexual sin or fornication. Likewise, private, public and religious discourse is quick to examine the perfunctory duties of sex, but fails to

5. Ibid., 123.

6. Ellison and Brown Douglas, *Sexuality and the Sacred*, 69.

7. Ibid.

8. Ibid.

9. Ibid., 70.

make those distinctions that make one spiritual in all areas of life, including sex life. The negative impact of sexuality and spirituality are also reflected in the painful history of slavery and African American women. Kimberly Wallace-Sanders, in *Skin Deep, Spirit Strong: The Black Female Body in American Culture*, describes the dichotomy of Black women in American culture and the legacy of slavery. Black women "manifested themselves in two distinct and paradoxical stereotypes—they were disgustingly lustful (Jezebel, according to historian Deborah Gray White) but exceptionally unfeminine . . . alluring but unattractive; they attracted and repelled at the same time."[10] Katie G. Cannon, in "Sexing Black Women: Liberation from the Prisonhouse of Anatomical Authority," sums up the dehumanization of Black women's bodies:

> In order to inscript our skin that is "too dark," our hair that is "too nappy," our facial features that are "too broad," and our buttocks that are "too wide," as definitive loci of positive human beingness, Black churchwomen are taught that we must suppress the sexual aspect of our humanity, by reinforcing norms and practices that proclaim procreational sex as a gift from God and relational, recreational sex as the devil's handiwork.[11]

These depictions are painful reminders of African American women and the manner whereby; they have been defined by others and have wrestled with the divine and spiritual from within and without. The paradox of these beliefs are contradicted in African cultures "that celebrated sexuality and spirituality and resisted the dualistic distinctions between the sacred and the secular, the soul and the body."[12] African traditions embodied a holistic approach to life while celebrating the divine and all that made one divine including their humanity, sex, sexuality and spirituality. According to African traditions, all aspects of humanity are "good," "acceptable" and "pleasing" because of the sacred and divine from within and without, including "Black skin" as an embodiment of the divine and sacred. However, Christianity inherited Euro-American and Puritanical beliefs that the body is overcome by a "higher and transcended power that is rational and spiritual."[13] Furthermore, this split of sexuality and spirituality also catapulted the notion of True Womanhood respectability where White females

10. Wallace-Sander, *Skin Deep Spirit Strong*, 23.
11. Cannon, "Sexing Black Women," 79.
12. Ibid.
13. Ibid.

possessed the moral characteristics of wifehood, motherhood and sexual chastity, while Black women possessed none of these characteristics.[14] Slavery depicted Black women (and men) as chattel and property and therefore Black women (and men) did not possess the virtues and beauty like those in White society. As a result, there is the challenge of African American women and the fear of being perceived as falling into old sexual myths and stereotypes. What follows is that African American women are perceived as sexually immoral because of the legacy of slavery. On the other hand, there is the interpretive lens of the Black church that challenges sex as a sacred and precious gift from God.

This is particularly evident and challenging in the lives of SAACW. Sexuality and sexual expression are perceived as a distinctive problem for Christian singles of all age ranges. The Black church has limited dialogue on a practical sexual ethic for Christian singles. Discussions are usually crafted and geared toward a young adolescent group on the dangers of premarital sex, pregnancy, venereal diseases and other health risks. However, there is limited discussion that encompasses the needs of an older single population or other diverse populations of Christian singles. Most certainly, there is sparse dialogue on a healthy sexual ethic for all Christian singles and for those Christian singles that choose to live a less restrictive sexual life. Instead, Christian singles are lumped into one homogenous sexual age group. There is a difference in a young adolescent Christian single group versus a midlife Christian single group. Overall, the requirements of this homogenous Christian single group are as follows: they are to remain chaste until they are married and they are to sexually abstain if they are sexually engaged because this is what God spiritually and morally requires of them. However, the leap from singlehood to marriage is a very long leap for some Christian singles.

There is the closeted Christian single female population that is sexually active in an age of cultural hyper-sexuality while at the same time grasping for scriptural references to uphold their hyper-spirituality. It proves that it's difficult to deny one's body and sexual-spiritual being. Those who fall into the cultural demands of hyper-sexuality are considered "loose" and those who fall into the religious hyper-spirituality are considered "holier than thou." Kelly Brown Douglas illustrates the ethos and attitudes of the Black church; she asserts that "Black women are expected to remain chaste after joining the church, while the sexual conduct of Black men is condoned in

14. Ibid.

the Black church."[15] She explains the "humiliating sexist rituals where Black women and especially unwed mothers are chastised and made to repent in front of the whole congregation, while the fathers are often ignored."[16] Amid all of these factors, Black women's sexuality is deemed overly sexual and therefore certain Black congregations require Black women to cover their legs with lap cloths and their heads with head cloths to keep them from distracting men while at the same time covering their sexual sin.[17] While she speaks about the ethos of the Black church and does not mention this statement specifically for Christian singles of any age, it does allude to how African American men and women, single and married are represented in the Black church. It also speaks to the sexual polarity that exists between African American men and women from the teachings of the Black church. My research participants discuss the matter of sexual choice and the two polarized worlds of sexuality and spirituality in their *Narratives of Sexuality and Spirituality*.

Narratives of Sexuality and Spirituality

> Diane, age 43: I think that I am normal. I've had sex outside of marriage with boyfriends. But at this point in my life I know how physicality and spirituality work; I know that it takes a lot of work to be sexually active with someone that you may or may not plan on having a life with. It takes something away from your spirituality. I think I have just gotten to the point in my life where I understand that whole ripping away thing. It's more than just we just broke up and we are not together anymore, it's a spiritual intertwining and after you keep ripping that away so many times, for me I'm done, it's not worth it. The sexual gratification is not worth the entanglement and having to go through the grieving process because it's a spiritual entanglement again, again, and again. So I'm tired of that. Because I know what that feels like it's actually made it easy for me to not be sexual because even though I want to be, I know what it means. And I don't want to feel that in my soul and spirit, the entanglement and then the ripping away. It's more than merging with someone physically it's merging your spirit and flesh. Even though it feels good and it's great, everything after that

15. Ibid.
16. Ibid., 83.
17. Ibid.

you have to deal with in terms of your heart, emotions. That's too much and I decided that I don't want to do that anymore.

Angie, age 48: To be honest, I don't have any sexual needs right now. For me sex I can take it or leave it because I was a virgin until I was 35 years old. It's not like I absolutely need sex and at this point I can live with it or live without it. This is where I am right now. There is a struggle with the church and me being a pastor. I have to walk a fine line. But I decided that I can do what I want with my body. Sex is between me, my partner and God and ultimately that's who I have to give accountability to. I don't have inhibitions of having sex outside of marriage as a single woman. I don't believe it's a violation of my faith. I just only require that if I'm going to be in a sexual relationship that I'm intelligent about it, that I know the person really well, that this is the person that I love, respect and there's a possibility of it going further, and any person that I'm involved with they have to be open to real and honest conversation. Because knowing that I am a pastor they have to be a person that respects privacy and discretion because I know not everyone in the church is going to embrace that.

Tracy, age 53: Needs, I don't know that I have needs, but I would call it a desire because I trust God to supply all my needs. And I have everything I need, do I have everything I desire, no. Do I want to be with a man physically? Every 30 seconds, I'm always looking. I've been there and I know what that feels like. I know what good sex is and I know what not so good sex is. And what I have learned, since the last time I've had sex which is probably four years ago, I've learned that without the total package sex is useless, I need love real love, I don't need lust—I need love. I need someone that connects with me more than in the bedroom. I need for the person to care intimately for me, because his lovemaking will come from that place. The sexual act will come from that place and I can discern the difference.

For religious, social, moral and personal reasons, Diane, Angie and Tracy have certain sexual ethics and choices that govern their lives. Diane and Angie have enjoyed an active sex life and are in sync with their sexual needs. But they also have encountered some hurt and disappointment in their sexual encounters. Diane's sexual encounters felt similar to marriage, an "intertwining" of the physical, emotional, psychological and spiritual. The break-up of her relationships felt like a divorce, "a ripping away," followed by grief and loss. Sex is a "merging of the flesh, soul and spirit," a physical connection; a spiritual and cognitive connection. At this time, Diane is abstaining from sex because there is "a lot of emotional work" involved in sharing her sex, body, mind and spirit.

Tracy has similar views about her sexuality and spirituality. Although she would like sex on a regular basis, casual sex without an intimate connection, the "total package" is not worth her investment. The difference between "good and bad sex" is the love and intimacy that she is able to "discern" within herself and from her sexual partner. The sexual wisdom is the knowledge and understanding that sex and intimacy begin with love, value and respect outside of the bedroom and lovemaking. As noted earlier in this discourse, sexuality and spiritually are "more than what we do with our genitals . . . it is an intimate communication human and divine."[18]

Angie "can do what she wants with her body." She doesn't deny or suppress her sexuality, but she is "discrete" with her sexuality as leader and pastor in the church. Angie's narrative illustrates the splitting of the sexual and spiritual and the paradoxical nature that takes place in trying to uphold the strict and legalistic stance of the church juxtaposed with honoring her sexual expression as a single woman. Angie respects her body as sex is not something that she does haphazardly, but she thinks intelligently about her sexual partners and her sexual decisions. Although Angie did not have sex until much later in life, her sexual needs are at minimum at this time. Sex is something that she can "live with" or "live without." Angie defines sex as an intimate connection with herself, her partner and God. It is not a "violation of her faith," but one which informs and honors her faith as a spiritual and sexual human being.

Thus, sexuality and spirituality are connected to sexual ethics, sexual choice and sexual freedom. Diane, Angie and Tracy made sexual choices that were well thought out and right for them. Moreover, they loved themselves in the midst of their choices. They were able to take a step back to reflect about their sexual needs and realized that they needed more than physical contact. They did not deny their sexuality, sensuality and spirituality despite living in the tension of the church.

18. Ibid., 18.

THE SEXUAL MYTH OF VIRGINITY AND FORNICATION

Virginity and fornication are the Ten Commandments for the female body and moral character. The biblical commandments on the female body and sexual purity equate virginity with godliness and fornication with uncleanness. As a young girl, the central sexual message reiterated by the church mothers was, "Keep your legs closed!" This was interpreted by me to mean several things: "act like a lady," "keep your dress down," "don't have sex," "don't get pregnant" and "remain a virgin until you are married." It said something about my embodiment as a young girl and that sex was restrictive and dangerous. Even more, as a budding young girl, I was constantly reminded of my shape, the expanse of my breast, hips and buttocks. The body shame, guilt and sexual innuendo that followed these conversations were challenging to comprehend. I somehow interpreted those messages to mean that my body was off limits to me and others in the community. I grew up thinking that if I did not follow these commandments, I offended God and those I cared about in my community. Thus, there is a major emphasis on maintaining one's status as a virgin while not committing the offensive act of fornication. Other distinctions are outlined below.

At the apex of proper female etiquette and sexual decorum is virginity. Virginity is the status of not having had a sexual relationship and it is the symbol of purity and holiness in Christian and religious circles.[19] Virginity is derived from the Latin word, *virgo*, which means "a female created for a male."[20] Although there are male virgins, virginity in its inception is synonymous for females. Jana Marguerite Bennett references an Augustinian perspective in *Water Is Thicker Than Blood: An Augustinian Theology of Marriage and Singleness*: "Virginity is a state of life that allows one to live without spot or blemish,"[21] reminiscent of the church's position and marital relationship to Jesus Christ. So, the perception of virginity is one that is held in high esteem both physically and spiritually.

Historically, women in the Judaic-Christian tradition were expected to uphold a standard of purity and were forbidden from participating in premarital sex. Jeopardizing their virginity meant the kiss of death. Furthermore, women who disavowed premarital laws and commandments were considered "defiled," "deflowered," "tainted" or "damaged goods" indicative

19. Tavassoly, "Virginity," 874.
20. Ibid.
21. Ibid., 91.

of their fallen state in the eyes of God and in the life of their community. Women were considered property and had no value if they were sexually impure. This is clearly evident in the narrative of Tamar (2 Sam 13:1–29). Tamar, daughter of David, was raped by her half brother Amnon and was forced to live as a desolate and fallen woman without the possibility of marriage or children because she was no longer a virgin. Through no fault of her own and as a survivor of rape, Tamar was forced to live on the margins of her community as a sexually defiled woman.

Mary the mother of Jesus lived in the periphery of her community for similar yet different reasons. The centrality of the New Testament is based on the Virgin Mary and Christ's birth (Matt 1:18–25 and Luke 1:26–38) into the world. Christ was conceived by the Holy Spirit with the assistance of the chosen vessel Mary. How this impacted the social milieu of that day and the implications of a young virgin girl betrothed to Joseph, conceiving without his consent and without having had sexual intercourse was and is difficult to fathom. Just how could a young girl conceive without having sexual contact? From the biblical accounts, we don't know all that transpired in the community with this announcement of a virgin conception and birth, but we know that Mary and Joseph had a reputation to uphold. However, the perceived dalliance of Mary meant death in a culture that had a number of social values, especially for women.

The cultural perceptions during this time period were based on perceived gender roles and these roles were interpreted through a lens of honor and shame where men had "precedence over others, established chiefly through one's ability to achieve physical, economic, or political dominance" and women "by their very nature were the weaker sex"[22] and were confined to space within the home. Both men and woman were expected to honor their families name and reputation and not shame or disavow that name. In the same way, the concept of virginity and the honor and shame motif is prevalent today. There is a double standard in religious circles where women are expected to carry the virginity "badge of honor" while men are not necessarily held to this standard.

Just as virginity is held in high esteem, fornication is akin to sexual sin. Fornication is "any type of illicit sexual activity . . . Old Testament includes seduction, rape, sodomy, bestiality, certain forms of incest, prostitution (male and female) and homosexual relations . . . New Testament includes almost any form of sexual misconduct (that is, sexual activity outside the

---

22. Ehrman, *New Testament*, 371.

marriage relationship) could be designated as fornication or 'immorality.'"[23] Fornication as translated in the Greek, King James Version means *"porneia"* from which we get the word pornography. It is any unsanctioned sexual intercourse.

Pauline ideology (1 Cor 6:12–20) defines fornication as a destructive force and sinful to the body. At all cost one should "flee or shun fornication because it is a sin to the body."[24] Paul took seriously the sex drive for the "Christian" single, the widow/unmarried and referenced "it is better to marry than to burn" with "desire, NRSV: be aflame with passion" (1 Cor 7:9).[25] Paul expected for single persons like himself to practice self-control in matters of the body and the sex drive. For those who did not practice self-control Paul stipulates marriage. To the married couple in cases of "sexual immorality," Paul admonishes that "each man/woman" should have his/her "own wife/husband" and that "each person already married should have or possess his or her own partner so that each one gives the partner her or his conjugal sexual rights" (1 Cor 7:3) and have mutual "authority over each other's bodies" (1 Cor 7:4).[26] Therefore, Paul's mandate for fornication is applied to both single persons and married couples. However, Paul speaks approvingly about the single unmarried person and virgin who is able to give their love, devotion and service to the Lord. They are "anxious" about the things of the Lord (1 Cor 7:32–33).

Old Testament and New Testament interpretations place a stringent value on sexual conduct and sexual purity. I use the term sexual myth in relation to virginity and fornication because there are subtle internalized messages that women receive about their bodies, value and self-worth. Myth, as defined by Edward P. Wimberly in *Recalling Our Own Stories: Spiritual Renewal for Religious Caregivers*, "refers to the way beliefs and convictions are constructed and how these constructions shape our lives and our behavior."[27] Because the Black church holds a very rigid stance on sex, sexuality and spirituality, the virgin construct is the most revered status encouraged for a Christian single population and especially Christian single women. The sexual myth of virginity and fornication is an ethical one because virginal women are morally conscious women who are praised for their sexual

23. Efird, "Fornication," 349.
24. Horsley, 1 *Corinthians*, 89.
25. Ibid.
26. Ibid., 97.
27. Wimberly, *Recalling Our Own Stories*, 4.

sacrifice. Conservative Christian teachings suggest that chaste women are perceived as "good" and fornicating women are perceived as "bad." This binary position sets up an "either/or" and "good/bad" dichotomy. Preadolescent young girls, adolescent young women, midlife women and senior women are susceptible to teachings that intersect morality with body theology. These teachings and body theology place value and legitimacy on women's ability to remain "pure," "chaste," and "virginal," similar to the roles of women in Judaic-Christian communities. It places women as objects in the use of their bodies and sexuality. Second, it does not foster a holistic view of all their abilities and capabilities as subjects and valued human beings in their own right. Women are forced to live up to the ideal of purity that makes them "bad' for engaging in sex or having multiple sexual partners outside the bonds of marriage. There are negative repercussions for this behavior. Sexual women are potentially labeled as "sluts" or "whores" for engaging in premarital sex and are viewed as "unladylike" in religious circles. While the sexual injunction for men is quite different, the sexual lives of women and the myths and beliefs that have shaped them are challenging.

SAACW have embedded beliefs about their sexuality that connect with their familial, communal and religious surroundings. Sexual myths about sexual purity are laden with commentary about sin. Fornicating women are "sinful" or "shameful" women who should repent for having sex. The paradox in all of this is that there are women (men) who are sexually engaged, yet what they do in the privacy of their homes is quietly kept because of the ridicule and perhaps the shame that is attached to this behavior. Yet, the world in which we live is very sexually liberated, but the religious response is to separate sexually and spiritually from the world and its enticement.

In addition to religious sexual myths that are imposed on church women in general, there is the social sexual discourse that impacts African American Christian women. Katie G. Cannon, in "Sexing Black Women: Liberation from the Prisonhouse of Anatomical Authority," states, "Individually and collectively, far too many African American Christian women restrict their sexual agency, by binding them with all kinds of biblical cords and ecclesiastical strings, in order to counter the age old, pervasive stereotypes of being either sexually insatiable wenches—virile, promiscuous, and lusty, or fat, jolly, neutered mammies."[28] African American Christian women are expected to uphold an epic of morality while at the same time depriving themselves of their sexual desires. Cannon explains further, "The

28. Ibid., 80.

value laden matrix of moral interruption"[29] that causes Black churchwomen to deny their sexuality from the perspective of Blanche Richardson's *Best Black Women's Erotica*:

> As women, so many of us are deprived of a healthy respect of and connection to our sexuality. For some it is shrouded in so much shame, by so many convoluted messages, that we become detached from our sexual identities. We like sex, but we can't talk about it. We engage in sex, but we are, at times, afraid to enjoy it. When we do enjoy the act, and our partners, we are often subjected to ridicule and heartbreak. It can get confusing and tiring. How can something so good, be bad for you? How can something that feels so good, cause so much pain?[30]

With the preponderance of a sexually liberating contemporary culture and a closeted sexually active church culture, is the answer in denying one's sexuality, or is it in embracing one's virginity or abstaining? How are messages being interpreted about maintaining one's virginity for marriage and what does this mean? What happens to women (men) who "fornicate" and don't live up to this expectation and how does God view this? These questions are explored in Diane, Angie's and Tracy's *Narratives of Virginity and Fornication*.

Narratives of Virginity and Fornication

> Diane, age 43: I felt angry at God because, the first time I had sex I was raped. I was eleven years old. And as I got older and heard people in the church say you can't have sex, I felt like God I didn't have a choice. It's not fair that I was tainted. I didn't go out to be tainted but I am. I never got to be that virgin saving myself for marriage. That wasn't an option. I felt like God this is really unfair because it's not like I had a chance to do that, so when people in church would try to guide and talk about sex I kind of listened, it was going in one ear and out the other because I was angry with God. That doesn't apply to me I didn't have a chance to decide to have sex or not have sex. And now I'm not a virgin and that's not fair.

29. Ibid.
30. Ibid.

Angie, age 48: As a pastor I try to present a very balanced and nonjudgmental view when it comes to sex and when we discuss sexual content in the Bible. Growing up in the church, I had one pastor who was adamant about everybody being married; he was anti-single you could just tell because he was always saying in Bible study it was better to marry than to burn. At the time I was growing up, so many young couples were dating, everybody was dating everybody. I was not in any of that—my pastor married a lot of people. One Sunday he presented his nephew and his nephew's pregnant finance in front of the church and he said "I told them they had to get married." I was so embarrassed for both of them; they looked embarrassed to me, to be brought in front of the church. She was obviously out to here and people were giving her the side eye. This was compounded by the fact that he was dating people in the church and this was a girl outside of the church. One young lady was so upset by it that she ran out of the church. And we all knew why because he had been dating her. So it created such tension and everyone was running around. It was almost a wedding every week literally. Now, most of the people are divorced or barely hanging on in their marriages. It was just so everybody had to get married. I look back on that experience and I wasn't a part of that stuff. I felt so bad for them and there was some marriages I know should not have taken place. They just didn't want to be single and the pressure in the church.

Tracy, age 53: When I was 17 and 18 years old a mother of the church said to me you are growing up and becoming a lady now and when you get pregnant, you let those babies come. And I knew that was not something she should have been saying to a 17- and 18-year-old girl, I was not sexually active—so at the church where I was raised I didn't have a lot of conversation. I wasn't fearful of sex. My church did not prepare me in that regard. They didn't have a stance either way there were a number of children born out of wedlock. That was more common than not. It was quietly condoned.

There are many collective messages about sex, virginity and fornication that are discussed in the Black church. Diane experienced a great deal of conflict in processing her sexual trauma in relation to the teachings of the Black church. Losing her virginity from rape, Diane had strong beliefs about her sexual status. She described herself as a "tainted" young woman, who didn't quite know where to place herself after her rape—internally within herself, with God or her community of faith. She was never going to meet the end goal of "saving herself for marriage." No amount of biblical teaching could explain the loss of her virginity in an act of violence and this fueled her anger against God. At all cost, Diane wanted to maintain this ideal image as a virgin because she believed that this is what God required of her and the Black church supported this belief. Her anger was as much against herself for not having control over what happened to her as it was against God for the shame and stigma that she still carries.

Angie's earlier recollections about virginity and fornication were based on the scriptural reference, "it's better to marry than to burn." The remedy for downplaying one's natural sexual urges and desires is marriage. This is illustrated with the pastor's nephew and pregnant fiancé. As noted, they were obviously sexually engaged with one another and forced to stand before their congregation with a scarlet letter etched on their foreheads and etched within her womb. They were condemned for having sex and their penance was marriage. Because of the scriptural reference "it's better to marry than to burn," many of Angie's peers married as a means of controlling their sexual desires while others married because they could not cope with their own feelings of loneliness. Marriage in many cases did not solve the problem of fornication, loneliness or other marital expectations as indicated by the number of divorces. It suggests that it takes more than just sex and a marriage certificate to make a relationship come together or to determine the longevity of the relationship. The rush to the altar is now compounded by the religious stigma of divorce alongside sexual myths and marital fulfillment. As a pastor, Angie now tries to present a "balanced" and "nonjudgmental view" on sex and sexuality to her congregation.

As well, Tracy's sexual recollections were conflictual because she was given permission to have sex and babies by a church mother. This is usually antithetical to what is publicly taught in the Black church about maintaining one's virginity; yet Tracy was given the green light by an older church mother. This certainly brought up for Tracy conflictual questions and feelings of distrust with other women, God and faith. Her statement typifies the sexual overtones that African American women and young African American girls face even in the Black church and society. Second, these perceptions and others were not counterbalanced with discussions on sex and sexuality despite the number of young men and women who had "children out of wedlock." Tracy states, sex was "quietly condoned" and a taboo subject in her church except in this one incidence with the church mother.

Tracy wishes that her church had given her more guidance so that she was prepared sexually in the world.

For this reason, there are numerous beliefs about sex and sexuality that are conveyed to African American women. Sexual myths have been used to appropriate women's sexuality and African American women's sexuality in various aspects. Diane, Angie and Tracy have debunked many of the sexual myths that have shaped and informed their beliefs as young girls growing up in the Black church. As SAACW, they have learned to intersect the moralistic virtues of the Black church with their own interpretations and embodiment as sexual women.

MASTURBATION

Another important aspect of sex and sexuality is self-gratification and self-stimulation that is embarrassing and uncomfortable to discuss publicly. There is a religious taboo that is attached to masturbation because it is associated with sexual pleasure. Sex has been traditionally connected to procreation according to the biblical rite, but what about sexual pleasure, sexual fulfillment and sexual climax? The evidence of sexual pleasure and sexual fulfillment is canonized in the Hebrew Bible, Song of Songs where the passion, excitement and the erotic pleasures of sex are poetically outlined. However, if the Black church does not allow premarital sex and if individuals choose to "service themselves" in this way, what does this mean? Historically, religion viewed masturbation as an "ungodly" act. Similarly in psychoanalytical discourse masturbation has been viewed as a contributor of "neurosis." These religious and psychological perceptions are further examined.

The *Dictionary of Pastoral Care and Counseling* defines masturbation as "sexual arousal caused by self-stimulation—from the Latin root *manus* (hand) and *stuprare* (to defile)."[31] Although the Bible does not specifically address masturbation, Gen 38:8–10 has been used to illustrate the sinful nature of masturbation through the interpretation of Onan. Onan was slain by God for spilling his seed. In Judaic-Christian circles, many people have interpreted this text to mean that Onan masturbated, sinned and therefore was slain by God. However, Onan's sin was not spilling his semen on the ground (coitus interruptus) but was a failure to fulfill Levitical law.[32] Religious views lean toward procreational sex and any sex out-

31. Phipps, "Masturbation," 691.
32. Ibid.

side of this premise is viewed as sinful and corruptible. Thomas Aquinas "classified masturbation as an unnatural sin more deserving of damnation than the natural sins of rape, incest, and adultery, where procreation was a possibility."[33] Sigmund Freud interpreted masturbation from Victorian standards in which masturbation "vitiates the character through indulgence and that it might result in diminished potency in marriage. . . . Masturbation was the cause of a neurosis characterized by fatigue, worry, and lack of physical and mental alertness."[34]

From a clinical perspective, masturbation has also been linked to physical and mental dysfunction whereby the frequency causes physiological and neurological problems. However studies today indicate that masturbation is a "harmless sexual activity that releases tension/stress" and is an "enjoyable expression of sexuality."[35] For males and females, masturbation helps to alleviate sexual tension in several ways: "some women find it a relief for menstrual cramps, it can transform a restless night into a quiet sleep and it can be an aid to restoring physical energy."[36] The point here is that the sex drive is influenced by biological, psychological and social factors. For some, masturbation is a powerful sexual expression for experiencing an orgasm.

For SAACW, masturbation is a form of sexual expression. Some may prefer to gratify themselves in this manner over and against having a sexual partner. Some may prefer not to masturbate and would rather sexually engage with a sexual partner. Some will not approach either stance as it is a violation of their Christian faith. The crux of the matter is that sexual wholeness, sexual freedom and sexual enjoyment has a multiplicity of expressions; however, some expressions are independent of others. Some SAACW may find sexual pleasure in fulfilling their sexual and bodily needs. As examined throughout this discourse, sexuality is embracing one's innate sexual desires and those desires are intrinsic to what makes one human. I believe that masturbation, as are all types of sexual expression, is important to sexual discourse because it speaks about being in tune with one's sexual body, sexual needs and desires. Masturbation is also viewed as an alternative "closeted" indulgence that has a minimal risk for pregnancy and venereal disease. Yet, it carries a high risk of moral condemnation.

33. Ibid.
34. Ibid.
35. Ibid.
36. Ibid.

Whether or not masturbation is an acceptable or unacceptable form of sexual pleasure is reflected upon by Diane, Angie and Tracy in the *Narratives of Masturbation*.

Narratives of Masturbation

> Diane, age 43: I don't agree with it. Because you can't just masturbate, you have to conjure up some imagery. It's not just you and yourself. I think I feel about masturbation the way I feel about drugs, they help and sedate temporarily. But the issue is still there and it doesn't solve anything. That's my opinion.

> Angie, age 48: The church view is that it is absolutely sinful. For me it was something for a long time I believed I wouldn't do it—I'm never going to do it. I don't do. Now I don't see it as a sinful thing for people that do and for people to service themselves in that way. That really only changed from seminary because I was absolutely against it. So seminary helped to enlighten me in that process. I would try to be supportive of whatever people decided to do and whatever happens what you do with your body is between you and God and you have to reconcile that for yourself.

> Tracy, age 53: It's not fulfilling. It is strictly the flesh for me, when I feel need to be taken care of in that way. I get quiet it's strictly biological. If I succumb to that I'm so through with me. And afterwards it's like having bad sex, sex with the wrong person, because it's not what I want. I want love and I want intimacy, I can't be intimate with me. Part of the intimacy is the element of surprise. I got to tell myself which way to move, which way to touch, so it's almost like mutilation to me. It's not pretty. It really isn't. I don't feel good—yes that thing is off that thing inside of my flesh, but I don't feel good.

The thought of sexual gratifying oneself is a difficult to grasp for Diane, Angie and Tracy. Diane is uncomfortable with the mental exchange and the transient sexual pleasure that is derived from masturbating. In order to reach an orgasm, one has to "conjure" some imagery or fantasy and Diane doesn't like this process. Masturbation takes care of a sexual need, but it does not "solve" all relational desires that one may have. Diane compares masturbation to a drug that temporarily anesthetizes the sexual urge.

In the past, Angie had similar views about masturbation and its "sinful" nature. In the course of seminary training and critical reflection, Angie is now of the mind-set that masturbation is not "sinful" for those persons who chose to enjoy this type of sexual expression. Although masturbation is not her personal preference, she believes it is a personal choice between the individual and God. More importantly, what you do sexually with your body is a sacred personal choice. People have to reconcile their differences and beliefs with God and not necessarily with the church. Maybe God enlightens in the midst of discovery as Angie encountered in her seminary training. Her approach is to invite God in the conversation, in all aspects that make one human, sexual and spiritual, including masturbation.

Tracy hasn't quite reached the point where she totally embraces masturbation. In fact, she experiences shame, guilt and "doesn't feel good" about herself when she does masturbate. On the one hand it takes care of her sexual needs and on the other hand it makes her feel bad. She lives in this good and bad dichotomy—the split of the sexual and spiritual—the sinful nature of her bodily sexual needs. Tracy describes masturbation in a variant of ways: "unfulfilling," "mutilation," "that thing inside my flesh," "bad sex" and "wrong person." In some respects masturbating makes her feel damaged, ruined, cut off, alienated or other body. She doesn't feel liberated or enjoys responding to her bodily needs. Instead, Tracy desires to experience intimacy with a sexual partner.

Although masturbation is not the typical form of sexual expression for Diane, Angie and Tracy, to some extent it fulfilled some sexual needs (at least for Tracy but questionable for Diane). What is noted is that masturbation is still very complicated and carries with it a social, moral and religious stigma. Similar to the earlier religious convictions which characterized masturbation as "sinful," "damnable" or a "disturbance of one's character," masturbation is still considered a disgrace. For some, it may "sedate temporarily", but it does not necessarily "feel good" emotionally or psychologically. Tracy's narrative sums up best the pathology that is attached to masturbation, she denotes, "if I succumb to that, I'm so through with me." Masturbating may fulfill a "fleshly" need but it does not necessarily make any of these women feel good in the internal process.

CONCLUDING THOUGHTS

This chapter opened with reflections on sex, sexuality and spirituality that are governed by social, gender, religious realties and sexual myths. To be sure, there is tension between the sexual and the spiritual, the secular and the sacred. These tensions were examined in critical reflections on virginity, fornication and masturbation with an overarching discourse on sexuality and spirituality. As espoused throughout this chapter, sexuality and spirituality are intrinsic to all that makes one human, divine and sexual.

Chapter 6

A Womanist Theological and Biblical Image of Singleness

"Mary and Martha"

Womanist theology evaluates, reevaluates and reflects upon the realities, traditions and practices of African American women through the lens of Scripture and biblical interpretation. The nuance of womanist theology is that it draws from a myriad voices, relations and experiences of African American women and women of color. Womanist theology "offers opportunities for Black women to feel fully participative in the theological processes and dialogues."[1] There are notable womanist theologians and scholars who highlight the experiences of African American women from many vantage points.

Delores S. Williams, in *Sisters in the Wilderness: The Challenge of Womanist God Talk*, examines the narrative and life of Hagar (Gen 16: 1–16 and 21:9–21) and the parallelism between the Hagar's situation and "African American's women's predicament of poverty, sexual, and economic exploitation, surrogacy, domestic violence, homelessness, rape, motherhood, single parenting, ethnicity, and meetings with God."[2] In *White Women's Christ, Black Women's Jesus: Feminist Christology and Womanist Response*, Jacquelyn Grant challenges the dualistic terms of Christ and Jesus as it is appropriated within feminist and womanist modes of religious thinking. Kelly Brown Douglas, in *Sexuality and the Black Church: A Womanist Per-*

1. Mitchem, preface to *Womanist Theology*.
2. Williams, *Sisters in the Wilderness*, 5.

spective, elaborates on the Black church, sexuality and Black sexuality from historical and current lenses. She also challenges the resistance and limited sexual discourse within the Black church. Womanist Ethicist, Emilie M. Townes *In a Blaze of Glory: Womanist Spirituality As Social Witness* explores womanist spirituality as "embodied," "personal," and "communal."[3] Teresa Fry Brown examines African American women and the spiritual values as handed down from grandmothers, mothers and other mothers in *God Don't Like Ugly: African American Women Handing on Spiritual Values*. Carroll A. Watkins Ali's work *Survival and Liberation: Pastoral Theology in African American Context* offers a womanist pastoral theological construct and a new paradigm in relation to the communal needs of the African American community that utilizes the cultural resources from within the African American community. Womanist theologians borrowed many of its womanist hermeneutical lenses from Alice Walker's groundbreaking term *womanist*, which integrates a myriad of expressions that are specific to the embodiment, traditions, spirituality, care and practices of African American women and the communities in which they serve.[4] Therefore, I will reference a womanist theological image of Mary and Martha (Luke 10:38–42) as interpreted from feminist scholarship and I will integrate my own womanist pastoral theological voice to explore singleness from the voices of SAACW.

MARY AND MARTHA: A FEMINIST INTERPRETATION, CHALLENGING GENDER ROLES

The Gospel of Luke 10:38–42 offers an interesting view of two single women living together and sharing resources and it gives a diverse imagery of a household that is not the typical "coupled" familial households that are portrayed in early antiquity. The narrative begins with a hospitable gesture of welcome by Martha the mistress of the household to Jesus and his disciples.

> Now as they went on their way, he entered a certain village, where a woman named Martha welcomed him into her home. She had a sister named Mary, who sat at the Lord's feet and listened to what he was saying. But Martha was distracted by her many tasks; so she came to him and asked, "Lord, do you not care that my sister has left me to do all the work by myself?" Tell her then to help me."

3. Ibid., 3.
4. Walker, "Womanist," in *In Search of Our Mothers' Gardens*, xi–xii.

> But the Lord answered her, "Martha, Martha, you are worried and distracted by many things; there is need of only one thing. Mary has chosen the better part, which will not be taken away from her. (Luke 10:38–42 NRSV)

Feminist scholars challenge the specific gender-related roles in this account. Two distinct images and dichotomies are noted. According to Jane Schaberg, in the *Women's Bible Commentary*, "Popular literature and traditions associated with Martha give evidence that many women have been long uncomfortable with this familiar story, which pits sister against sister."[5] This premise is also supported by Elizabeth Schüssler Fiorenza in *But She Said: Feminist Practices of Biblical Interpretation*. Schüssler Fiorenza suggests the dualistic patriarchal reading of the Luke not only "restricts women's ministry and authority but also reinforces societal and ecclesiastical polarization of woman."[6] Luke uses the term *diakonia* which correlates with eucharistic table service, proclamation, and ecclesial leadership.[7] In the first century CE many leaders and founders of house churches were women and therefore would have fulfilled these *diakonia* roles. Martha as mistress of the house has an authoritative *diakonia* role. Luke, however, challenges this perception and presents to his readers a more passive role for women (Mary), while admonishing an active role of women in the context of ministry, authority and leadership (Martha). Schüssler Fiorenza purports that Martha's complaint to Jesus is not against having too much work, but rather being denied her proper ministerial role and authority. The implication of reading this text from a patriarchal lens is that women are denigrated for their work while at the same time relegated to traditional roles and responsibilities as their proper place. Moreover, women are expected to fulfill these insurmountable "double roles" as "super women."[8] Schüssler Fiorenza expounds on what she terms the "good woman / bad woman dichotomy—women ought to be not only good disciples but also good hostesses, not only ministers but good housewives, not only well paid professionals but glamorous lovers."[9] Schüssler Fiorenza recommends a "hermeneutics of creative imagination and ritualization that articulates alternative liberating interpretations that do not build on the andocentric dualisms and patriar-

5. Schaberg, "Luke," 376.
6. Schüssler Fiorenza, *But She Said*, 68–69.
7. Ibid., 377.
8. Ibid.
9. Ibid.

chal functions of the text."[10] This is done through a retelling and revisioning of Mary and Martha that moves away from alienating one sister from another. My interpretation of Luke 10:38–40 is explored from a womanist retelling and imagination in the context of SAACW.

MARY AND MARTHA: A WOMANIST INTERPRETATION, BRIDGING TWO WORLDS

How might a womanist interpretation rework some of the roles, perceptions and biblical images that have shaped SAACW and their understanding of singleness? The Gospel of Luke is written in a time period where women were not treated as intellectual equals to their male counterparts and were relegated to the female space within the home. However, the Lukan writer gives prominence to Mary and Martha as women are usually unnamed and unidentified in the Bible. As noted with Schüssler Fiorenza, many interpretations "pit" one sister against the other sister. At the onset, Mary and Martha are searching to find their place in the midst of many roles and interpretations of womanhood in the culture. Martha is the antagonist, "identified problem" and the sister who doesn't quite measure up with the service that she provides. Mary, however, is the "golden child" who at least for the moment is doing what is required of her as she leaves the service for something "better" that involves sitting, listening and learning from Jesus. One sister is good because she has found the "better part" and another sister is bad for not finding the "better part." Yet, both women have unique gifts, talents and interest.

> Now as they went on their way, he entered a certain village, where a woman named Martha welcomed him into her home. She had a sister named Mary, who sat at the Lord's feet and listened to what he was saying. But Martha was distracted by her many tasks; so she came to him and asked, "Lord, do you not care that my sister has left me to do all the work by myself?" Tell her then to help me." But the Lord answered her, "Martha, Martha, you are worried and distracted by many things; there is need of only one thing. Mary has chosen the better part, which will not be taken away from her." (Luke 10:38–42 NRSV)

What does it mean for SAACW to manage their necessities in the twenty-first century? SAACW are the sole providers for their households

10. Ibid., 73.

without financial, emotional and physical support from husbands. Many may rely on varied support from their extended families, but overall they don't have the luxury of meditating with Jesus at the expense of not working and jeopardizing their jobs. If they "sat" without working how would they maintain their livelihood or pay their bills? *Martha complains to Jesus "Lord, do you not care that my sister has left me to do all the work by myself?" "Tell her then to help me."* The reality of SAACW is that there are no husbands to subsidize their living expenses and therefore education, salaries and careers are essential for their survival. The life of SAACW is dependent upon a moderately healthy lifestyle and economic stability to maintain their livelihood. Working could be interpreted as a "distraction" but it is also as a means of survival in life.

Martha was angry, frustrated and resentful toward Mary for not assisting her, but Mary is said to have "*chosen the better part which will not be taken away from her.*" What does it mean for a woman in the Greco-Roman culture to take her place with disciples and the master teacher Jesus? It means a claiming of autonomy and authority. Mary changed her routine from preparing and serving food for a different kind of sustenance, reflection and survival. Mary did not ask anyone's permission to claim her reflective time with Jesus and the disciples. We don't hear Mary's words but we hear her actions as she reclaims those parts of herself.

Similarly, SAACW reclaim their authority by naming and defining their personhood, womanhood and sustenance in life. Although work, education, career and ministry are important, there are intellectual, emotional, spiritual, psychological and sexual needs that sustain them as human beings. In reading this Lukan text, Mary chooses "the better part" but Martha has a "necessary part" that works in conjunction with Mary. I believe that both Mary and Martha are symbolic of the "*better parts.*" The reinterpretation of this text not only affirms all aspects of Mary and Martha, but it "blesses" all aspects of SAACW. In obeying the teachings of the Black church they deny those other sacred sexual parts of themselves because it is perceived as "sinful" to bless and affirm all needs that make them human. Some have made the decision to reclaim those necessary parts regardless of what anyone says, including the Black church. Others believe that they are "crazy" for having these feelings and they don't know what to do with their emotions and desires. So they sit and are frustrated, like Mary and Martha. Martha continues her service in frustration and Mary leaves her service because she is tired of the mundaness of life.

Mary and Martha are symbolic of the conflictual nature in which SAACW are forced to live. They are taught in the Black church to strengthen their spiritual minds and bodies, while sacrificing other important aspects in their lives. My womanist interpretation invites an integration and affirmation of both aspects of Mary and Martha because they represent the totality of spiritual, physical, emotional, sexual, intellectual and psychological needs that are important for their survival. SAACW work and serve inside and outside of their churches but have other needs that are important for their survival and existence. Instead of choosing one sister over the other or pitting one sister against the other, I see integrating all aspects of Mary and Martha as model of spiritual care. Both Mary and Martha have strengths and challenges but they represent a bridging, integration, balance and reclaiming of all aspects of their humanity and care.

A WOMANIST IMAGE OF JESUS WHO "WALKS ALONGSIDE"

In this study Diane and Tracy acknowledged that loneliness was a major struggle and the need for intimacy was felt strongly in certain pivotal moments. As Angie reflected back over her life she felt moments of regret and longings for children. Their concerns are similar to Martha's poignant question, *"Lord do you not care . . . ?"* SAACW are no different than the diverse individuals in the Bible who questioned God/Jesus about their current status and conditions in the world. After all, many of the psalmists complained and cried out to God about their current conditions and wondered if God had forsaken them? Jesus questioned his journey toward the cross in the garden of Gethsemane (Matt 26:36–46). Jesus prayed and asked God to "remove the cup." Jesus wrestled and struggled with the "cup" being representative of his purpose that led him to the cross, suffering, death and resurrection. To be sure, Jesus was fully human and fully divine and he went off by himself to reflect, question and I'm sure vent his anger and astonishment of the challenges he faced during his day. Thus, SAACW who are seeking husbands have similar "Gethsemane" moments and faith questions.

Martha's complaint to Jesus is fitting to numerous SAACW who complain about husbands, family and marriage. As Martha complained to Jesus about the lack of support from her sister Mary, some SAACW feel unsupported in their prayers and question if anyone cares, including Jesus, *"Lord do you not care . . . ?"* Who is Jesus and where is Jesus in the midst of their existential questions and relationship challenges? Working and managing their necessities in life is important; however, not having someone physically in their lives and in their beds is frustrating. Where are the men and the husbands who will share with them and provide steady companionship as interpreted from their biblical, social and familial lenses? How does this correlate with their understandings and perceptions of Jesus?

The Bible and sermonic moments are replete with images of marriage and family that are associated with the blessings of God, Jesus and Abraham. Historically, the Black church has been a strong familial institution where Black men and women worked collaboratively to accomplish a greater good and goal. Black men and women, both single and married, worked, served and prayed for their communities. Those who were single petitioned God for husbands, wives, families and marriages of their own because Black men and women were taught that *"Jesus is on the main line tell him what you want."* The theological premise behind this song is that whatever the need and whatever the concern, there is no problem too big or too small, Jesus can and does supply *all* of their needs, *fix* all of their problems, including petitions for husbands and wives. Thus, if a Black woman decided that she was ready to settle down, she could find potential prospects in the Black church. Nowadays, African American women continue their service within the Black church however; there is a decrease of African American men in the Black church to work alongside them. The current society is one where African American men and women struggle to maintain many of the core values and beliefs transmitted from the previous generations in what has been a cultural shift within the Black church and society. It is been stated that accomplishing academic goals has been a blessing and curse for SAACW who sacrificed securing a family for a career and education or who were limited in their dating and marriage prospects. As one church mother told me, "Baby, just because you wait to have a child or to get married later on does not mean that you will be able to." There is the complexity of finding suitable mates for today's single African American woman that was not an issue per se for some of the foremothers that served previously in the Black church. Thus, all of these complexities factor into the complaints and prayer lives of SAACW.

> Depending on the congregation, between 66 to 80 percent of its membership is usually composed of women. There are about 2.5–3 females to every male member. The usual anguished lament and questions heard from pastors and laity: "Where have all the Black

men gone? Why don't Black men attend church?" . . . A question that is often raised in discussions about the entry of women into positions of pastors and preachers in the Black church is whether the presence of women in leadership posts will drive away men.[11]

There are many reasons that are slated for the decrease of Black men in the Black church, and as stated above Black women are the "identified problem" as their leadership roles have served as the catalyst for the scarcity of Black men in the church. With that being said, today some SAACW never envisioned themselves single without partners to share in their successes, failures and accomplishments. This is a topic that continues to surface and resurface in the contemporary culture and within the African American community. While some "lament" over these challenges other SAACW have chosen to invest in themselves and live fulfilled lives and are not considering marriage, family or children. They have refused to put their lives or happiness on hold for the traditional marriage path that is found in the Black church, culture and society. Still others question the validity of God/Jesus in the midst of their uncertainty, fears, desires, sexual longings, aging, loneliness, aloneness and singleness. Not all SAACW experience these feelings and questions, but some do. Even I have similar questions as a professional, midlife single Christian African American woman who has many roles as an ordained minister, doctoral candidate, sister, daughter, granddaughter, aunt, great aunt and friend. With the demand and pull of all these polarities, I too wrestle with my own faith questions in the midst of my own loneliness, aloneness (at times) and desire for connection. Therefore, I ask, *"Lord do you hear me—Lord do you not care . . . ?"* I stand with other SAACW midlife and the tension of many spiritual, relational and existential questions. Therefore, how is Jesus interpreted in these existential moments for me and other SAACW? How would Jesus respond to the question *"Lord do you not care . . . ?"*

I invite SAACW to think about an image of Jesus as one who works with them and walks with them side-by-side as they journey through life. Singleness is a journey that evokes many embedded beliefs about Jesus as a rescuer and deliverer. However, Jesus who walks alongside does not rescue Martha from her predicament and neither does Jesus acknowledge her complaint in the way she expected. Neither does Jesus deliver or rescue SAACW from their isolating feelings nor does Jesus provide mates. Some SAACW are hopeful that their prayers and request have been heard

11. Lincoln and Mamiya, "Black Women, Black Men," 304.

and that Jesus will answer and send "the one" so that ideally some of their stressors in life are alleviated. But for many this is not the case. Dating and positioning themselves to meet potential partners is a source of frustration because many of their dating and relationship encounters fall short of marriage. The image of Jesus who walks alongside is not the Jesus who will answer every prayer request or satisfy every need. However, Jesus who walks alongside is one who challenges them as they make the necessary choices and decisions in life that might be antithetical to the teachings of the Black church, but not necessarily antithetical to the love, care and concern of God / Jesus Christ. I say this because the Black church has very few answers in how to accommodate a large population of its single female members. So they turn to faith, prayer, God and Jesus to find solace as they find clarity within themselves.

Jesus who walks alongside values their experiences and honors all aspects of their humanity. Singleness may seem trivial to some, but it is a concern for those women who desire love and companionship. Jesus embodies love and therefore manifesting that love is a human need and condition. If Jesus walks with African American women as they challenge patriarchal systems and racial oppression, then certainly Jesus walks with SAACW as they grapple with the relationship challenges within their communities. Furthermore, Jesus joins with them in their communal efforts to create a healthy environment in which they can thrive as single women.

When they are alone, lonely or hurting, Jesus works with them as they sort through their feelings that are a natural component of being human. Again, there are SAACW who don't lament over the fact that they are single, but they question the negative polarizations within the society. No, the image of Jesus who walks alongside does not *solve* all relationship problems or lessen the feelings of aloneness, loneliness or pain, but Jesus partners with them in the struggle.

Martha asks Jesus, *"Lord, do you not care that my sister has left me to do all the work by myself?" "Tell her then to help me." "But the Lord answered her, Martha, Martha, you are worried and distracted by many things; there is need of only one thing." "Mary has chosen the better part, which will not be taken away from her."*

What is the care that Martha needs and is seeking? Jesus' response invites Martha to define and discover for herself the care that she needs. As it turns out, the care that she seeks is the care that she can only identify. Likewise, Jesus invites SAACW to care for themselves in ways that are gratifying for them. But it also invites them to dialogue with their families and churches in how they desire to be treated, loved, respected and cared for. The Black church and the religious sector as a whole demands that single women live distinct asexual and moral lives until they are married. Yet, many SAACW are frustrated in trying to achieve this perfect image and are tired of limiting their potential because of the restrictions within the Black church. Some of these women will never marry, so they grapple with how to direct their lives in a holistic and healthy manner.

Some choose to participate sexually outside of the confines of marriage to fulfill sexual needs that are intrinsic to their humanity. Others choose different sexual paths including abstinence that are also indicative of their humanity. Still others desire love and find ways in which to fulfill these needs that affirm their worth and value as whole persons. Others in this group have established goals, dreams, self improvement and spirituality as a means of obtaining wholeness and care. Some move in other directions and chart new paths that are life-giving to their humanity. Yet, because they are human some will choose paths that are detrimental to their well being; however, Jesus stands with them in this process as well. Jesus does not make decisions for them and neither does Jesus choose their path. How they choose to live and what they choose to become is their decision. Jesus, who walks alongside, is one who extends free will.

As co-participants and co-creators in their care, SAACW exercise their freedom of choice. The invitation that Jesus extends to SAACW as co-participants challenges the image of Jesus who punishes or one who denigrates because of the freedoms that are explored by them. However, I believe that Jesus who walks alongside is one who cheers them on as they celebrate and make the necessary changes to achieve their happiness, liberation and fulfillment in life. Jesus leaves the final decision with Martha and admonishes her to find the "better parts" for herself. Mary finds her "better parts" in reflecting and listening to Jesus. The "better parts" is also reminiscent in a communal sense. Is it possible that Mary and Martha could have assisted each other to achieve the empowerment and freedom that they both desired in working collectively? In the same way, Jesus empowers SAACW to create the life that brings them freedom and empowerment. Moreover, Jesus invites them to discover their value and worth within themselves. Diane, Angie and Tracy speak about Jesus and God who walks with them in singleness in their *Narratives of Jesus and God in Singleness*.

Narratives of Jesus and God in Singleness

> Diane, age 43: I believe that Jesus is always there. When I talk to Jesus about my loneliness, Jesus always makes it a point to let me know that I'm not alone, ever. When I think about my loneliness I'm wishing as I go through life and experience things or have to deal with things that aren't so great, I wish it were someone there to hold my hand. But me not having that has showed me how Jesus is always there and how he always sends someone to be there for me. Because Jesus cares about something that I think is so small, I know he cares about it all.

> Angie, age 48: I feel like God is the co-creator in my singleness. I mean that I have the choice to be single but that choice is influenced by how I am made up. I think my purpose in being single is that God wants me to achieve something that I would not achieve or would be harder to achieve if I was tied to family and motherhood. It's something that kind of worked out that way.

> Tracy, age 53: I see God as supportive, companion, lover, the one that I share my heart. God is that person for me—husband like attributes, my expectation of what a husband should be—a provider. Somebody I can be myself with—those things I expect in a husband. We work together to make things happen. He can be whatever I need him to be in my life.

Diane, Angie and Tracy find comfort, purpose and support in knowing that Jesus and God journey with them. Diane has those critical moments where she questions, "*Lord do you not care . . . ?*" Jesus responds and says, "Yes I care." There are moments when she is lonely and frustrated, but Jesus reminds her that she is not alone. Jesus *cares* about all aspects of her life, be it small or large, and reminds her of this fact by sending support in times of need. For Angie, it's not about her experiences with loneliness but it is about her partnership with God to achieve a greater purpose other than marriage and family. She affirms that it's perfectly normal to embrace singleness. For Tracy, God has "husband-like attributes" in the support, love and care that God provides. She describes her relationship as a "working together" to accomplish her goals. Jesus and God empower Diane, Angie and Tracy to continue their journey as single women in transformative ways. Jesus and God worked with them in creating lives that are purposeful even in singleness.

IN CLOSING

This chapter integrates the experiences of SAACW with womanist theology and the biblical image of Mary and Martha. This chapter broadens the experiences of SAACW and some of the theological and existential challenges in life. Mary and Martha embody the work and service that many African American women provide to their churches and in their personal lives, yet there are other dreams and aspirations that they wrestle with daily. Mary and Martha represents the plight of singleness and how this too is a theological concern for many SAACW in the Black church. In many instances their spiritual, sexual, intellectual, physical, emotional and psychological needs are diminished in the service and work of God. However, the theological metaphor of Mary and Martha includes the diverse concerns of SAACW in their struggle to be heard in all aspects of life, including their relational life.

Chapter 7

"You Can't Just Treat Me Like a Stepchild"

RELATIONAL-CULTURAL THEORY AND HEALTHINESS OF THE SELF

Although it has been reiterated throughout this discourse that singleness is not a "sickness" nor does it make one "pathological," it is considered a social and religious stigma and it impacts the relational identity and self-acceptance of SAACW. Unmarried SAACW are categorized in many circles as lacking the ultimate marital relationships and therefore are denigrated for not having reached this cultural norm. Furthermore, some SAACW have internalized the belief that they are lacking somehow because they are single. All of these perceptions point to relational and cultural connections and disconnections. To be sure, the society and religion play a significant role in the images that signal one's "positive" or "negative" status within the social and religious milieu. There are representations and contemporary images that impact the relational development of African American women in the church and society. Despite their work and advancement in the dominant culture, they are still perceived as sexually promiscuous and this image that persists challenges their "worthiness" within themselves and within mainstream society, at times. Relational-cultural theory examines the "vital role that relationships and connectedness with others

play in the lives of women."[1] This is significant because women are social-
ized to develop their sense of self-worth and self-identity in context to their
relationships and connectedness with others. Moreover, relational-cultural
theory in its expansion includes the perspectives and relational experiences
of women of color and in particular African American women through
multicultural lenses. Therefore, this chapter will focus on relational-cultural theory and therapy as a social resource for SAACW and will be examined
for its therapeutic implications and as a means of exploring a healthy acceptance of the self.

RELIGION AND CULTURE: CONNECTION AND DISCONNECTION

A major emphasis in relational-cultural theory is in connections that foster
growth-enhancing relationships to others and the self, or what is called
self-in-relation.[2]

> This means that "for women, the primary experience of self is re-
> lational . . . the self is organized and developed in the context of
> important relationships" (Surrey, 1985, p.2). The model postulates
> that women's self development occurs within constructing, build-
> ing, and maintaining relationships where mutuality and reciproc-
> ity form the foundation of the relationship.[3]

A key component of therapy is the recognition that disconnections as
well as opportunities for growth occur not only on the individual and familial level, but on the sociocultural level. Relational-cultural theory examines
women's psychological development in the areas of difference, power and
privilege, as well as issues of racism, classism and sexism. Societal practices
of stereotyping greatly impact one's sense of connection and disconnection. Racism, classism and sexism hamper growth fostering relationships.
Relational-cultural theory posits that "an inner sense of connection to others is the central organizing feature of women's psychological development;
healing and growth are outcomes of connection, while pain, suffering, and

1. Herlihy and Corey, "Feminist Therapy," 368.

2. Brown and Root, *Diversity and Complexity*, 234.

3. Ibid., quoting Janet L. Surrey, *Self-in-Relation: A Theory of Women's Development*
(Wellesley College, MA: Stone Center, 1985).

psychological problems are outcomes of disconnection."[4] Jean Baker Miller worked collaboratively with several peers Judith Jordan, Irene Stiver, Janet Surrey and Clevonne Turner to what is also known as the Stone Center theoretical approach. Some criticisms of relational-cultural theory are that it lacked the diversity needed for women of color and women from other diversified groups. The founders, Baker Miller, Jordan, Stiver and Surrey, were limited to their White middle-class privilege status in which much of their clinical work was based upon. Therefore, Clevonne Turner expanded upon relational-cultural theory in naming the sociocultural lenses that are relevant in African American women's psychological development. There is an entirely different world and appropriate clinical applications that are important to their specific experiences and realities. Yvonne Jenkins, in "The Stone Center Theoretical Approach Revisited: Applications for African American Women," integrates Turner's work with her own therapeutic work with African American women. Jenkins denotes that "connection to or disconnection from African American heritage are central to how African American women perceive themselves and the world, how they cope, and their ability to move and take progressive action in the world."[5] A positive connection is developed through strong reinforcements in African American values that are developed from a lifelong exposure of experiences captured during their rearing. African American women whose rearing reinforced positive racial and cultural identities appear to have a higher regard of the self and social esteem. Jenkins denotes that they also have a more positive outlook in terms of their body image despite White societal polarization on standards of beauty. Because they utilize many of their familial, social and religious strengths, these women are able to withstand some of the discriminatory practices and oppression with their esteem intact, more so than those with fragile racial identities.[6]

In contrast, a negative disconnection develops from "internalized dominance/oppression that damages the connection to self and others."[7] With the history of slavery, African American women inherited many internalized beliefs about their intellectual abilities and acceptance of skin color that continues to be a source of contention in the African American community. Examples of disconnection for African American women include:

4. Jenkins, "Stone Center," 65.
5. Ibid., 69.
6. Ibid.
7. Ibid., 70.

"self hatred, poor body image, low self esteem, and low self confidence."[8] Other negative disconnections include: "self-defeating beliefs about one's possibilities of experiencing satisfying and fulfilling relationships, repeated romantic failures, and social isolation."[9]

Religion and spirituality are important to the legacy of African American women. The Black church has served as an esteem-building institution for African American women. As reiterated in relational-cultural theory, there are positive connections that are inherent in the African American tradition; however, there are also negative disconnections that work against SAACW in a communal sense as it influences perceptions on singleness, marriage and family. There is the paradoxical nature of the Black church as it speaks to the place, legitimacy and identity of single women. Diane, Angie and Tracy explain the dynamics that exist in their churches in the *Narratives of the Church Environment*.

Narratives of the Church Environment

Diane, age 43: When I go to church and I feel like my singleness is a disease that I have to maintain and live with until I get the cure— marriage. Being a part of a church as a single woman doesn't have to mean that I have this problem and eventually, hopefully, prayer- fully I won't have this single problem for too long. The church en- vironment is not safe sometimes.

Angie, age 48: My denomination focuses on the ministers spouses. As a single pastor, I am viewed with suspicion because I am not married and I don't have a spouse. The church wants everyone married so that's what the church promotes. My denomination certainly doesn't want me single at all. There has to be something wrong with me because I am not married or I can't find a husband. People think this about me all the time. They say, "Okay what is it? What's with her?" There has to be some kind of undercurrent reason, it can't be that I just want to be single. My reason is just not a good enough reason. They have to find me a husband or a boyfriend or something.

8. Ibid.
9. Ibid.

> Tracy, age 53: The Black church is responsible for developing
> healthy whole families. They can't leave me out because I am not
> married or I don't have a child because guess what I am a part of
> the family, your church family. You can't treat me like a stepchild
> and put me in a corner and pretend like I don't exist.

There is the complexity and psychological tension that exists for Diane, Angie Tracy as they describe three metaphors that capture their sense
of being and value within their places of worship: "disease," "suspicion" and
"stepchild." Diane is perceived as a problem—*diseased*. Angie's presence
is questionable—*suspicious*. Tracy is left out—the *stepchild*. They wrestle
against internalizing these messages and images that are promoted in their
churches. Despite how they are labeled, Diane, Angie and Tracy contradict
those aspects of the church the impact their self and social esteem. Diane
refuses to see herself as a "problem" that needs solving. Angie embraces
her singleness as an "acceptable" model of being despite the fact that her
denomination caters to ministers' spouses. Tracy pushes against her "in-
visibility" and secondary position and challenges the church's understanding of family and connection. "Healthy family" is one that includes single
women. Diane, Angie and Tracy's narratives call attention to significant
relational dynamics of single women and their connections and disconnections within the Black church. They challenge and even reject these evoking
images that impact their sense of health, "safety" and relational well-being.

In the Black church there exist some damaging perceptions of SAA-
CW as they are inundated with messages about marriage and the sacred
union of family in the most prominent hour, Sunday morning worship service. On the one hand they are members of this dynamic institution called
the Black church which has historically aided African American women in
finding meaning and hope within their complex struggles and hardships.
On the other hand, this dynamic institution has fostered some negative
perceptions of women, not to mention single women, in their legitimacy
as human beings. The dichotomy exists—they belong, yet they don't belong
because they are single and unmarried. SAACW are family and are a part
of the extended family that is evident in the Black church context, but un-
derneath the surface there is the subtle message that they need to hurry up
and marry so that they can become a part of this wholesome ideal image of
family that is portrayed in historic American society and that has infiltrated
the Black church. Relationally and psychologically it's like walking on egg
shells as SAACW are forced to live in this borderline relationship with the

Black church and its messages about family and belongingness. At times their relationship within the Black church is a positive move forward and at times their relationship with the Black church is a tenuous move backwards because of the systemic problems they face within this institution. A major focus for relational-cultural theory is engaging in growth-fostering relationships. The Black church has an opportunity to engage and build better relations with SAACW and SAACW can begin to engage and even challenge their roles and perceptions within the Black church.

RELATIONAL IMAGES AND STEREOTYPES OF SAACW IN MIDLIFE

There are destructive relational images in the society that impact African American women. According to relational-cultural theory, negative historical stereotypes and mythical images are damaging to African American women and the "relational image development of the population and society."[10] The impetus behind these negative representations is "racism and anxiety about difference."[11] Several images were examined in chapter 1: "You Must Be a Lesbian," "The Sinister Reason," "What's Wrong with You and Why Aren't You Married?," "How Old Are You?," "Miss Independent," and "I Choose—Single and Satisfied" all point to long-held beliefs, constructs and projections about African American women's sexuality and morality. African American women are perceived as sexually vile women without character. Although this discourse examines the plight of SAACW and their experiences in various social, familial and religious institutions, there is the "image problem" that haunts African American women and these images have an enormous influence in these institutions.

The following historical stereotypes and mythical images are examined: "*mammy*: a selfless caretaker, the epitome of trustworthiness, but also not very smart and often a buffoon, *matriarch*: strong, but domineering/controlling, *sapphire*: evil, bitchy, hard and tough, domineering, castrating, *she-devil/jezebel*: impulsive, promiscuous, seductive, and a loose woman/immoral, *welfare mother*: controlling, lazy, and irresponsible, *superwoman*: a strong workhorse, who values performance and achievement, does all things perfectly simultaneously, and has no needs of her own for

---

10. Ibid., 73.
11. Ibid.

interpersonal and sexual intimacy."[12] Although there is no monolithic image that captures the essence of African American women, negative images of African American women are imprinted in the contemporary culture.

For example, mammy is the nurturing woman who is desired because she is domesticated in her care of others but not in the care of the self (herself). Midlife "spinster" single women are characterized as nurturer's who are "undesirable" in their appearance, yet "desirable" in their care for others. The spinster single woman who cares for others is portrayed as very religious, submissive and asexual. The strong-willed, work-horse and castrating woman as characterized in the matriarch, superwoman, and sapphire mythical images are linked to the present day Miss Independent image in which single professional African American women are falsely perceived as strong, castrating and controlling in their hustle to acquire financial stability and educational and professional success. This also parallels with SAACW who utilize their power of choice to remain unmarried or uncoupled. Jezebel typifies the sexualized and objectified image that continues to haunt African American women from the legacy of slavery. SAACW are erroneously depicted as desperate women who live secret lives as lesbians and are sexually sinful as descendants of Eve. This image contrasts with the "spinster" single woman who is asexual and harmless. Most of all, the welfare mother incorrectly epitomizes all that is lacking and deficient in African American women. SAACW are portrayed as women who lack the necessary ingredients and social graces to attract marital relationships.

Thus, the psychosocial impact that historical stereotypes and mythical images has on the society and the identities of African American women is challenging. The implications of destructive historical stereotypes and mythical images are examined further from a relational-cultural perspective.

> African American women are portrayed as "sub-and superhuman beings who have "their place" that is, they are not to hold any authentic power or to be taken seriously, they are to be used and discarded, and they are fundamentally unacceptable. Stereotypes and mythical images disempower and oppress via (1) images that grossly distort the experiences, strengths, vulnerabilities, and potentials of African American women; (2) perpetuating internalizations that negatively impact development of self-other perceptions; and (3) fostering relational styles that perpetuate disconnection.[13]

12. Ibid.
13. Ibid.

The dichotomy exists for SAACW who are both African American and single. They are left with the difficult challenge in finding "their place" relationally in so many conflicting representations that impact the very essence of their womanhood. Relational-cultural theory posits that ongoing negative stereotypes could lead to a sense of self-doubt and feelings of unworthiness from fear of how others will respond to them.[14] Again, these types of feelings are dependent upon the values, wisdom and beliefs that have been instilled in them. Relational-cultural theory suggests that stereotypes and mythical images are catalysts for developing growth-fostering relationships via:

1. promoting accurate relational images of African American women,

2. social activism,

3. effective parenting and socialization of children,

4. articulating one's experiences, and

5. determination to not succumb to distortions and the disconnection these engender through bitterness, hopelessness, and social isolation.[15]

RELATIONAL-CULTURAL THERAPY AND HEALTHINESS OF THE SELF IN SINGLENESS

What is an appropriate healthiness of the self for SAACW in midlife? Relational-cultural theory is an inclusive model of therapy that addresses the relational experiences of women. "As a helping and healing counseling model, it identifies and deconstructs obstacles to mutuality that individuals encounter in diverse relational contexts and networks."[16] Relational-cultural therapy focuses on connections and disconnections that restrict and block psychic growth. The impetus for this approach is to find ways to move from disconnection to connection within the context of the therapeutic relationship. Moreover, relational-cultural theory and practice moves toward a healthy progression of psychological development rather than focusing on the pathological developments that are enforced in traditional psychoanalytic theories. The concept of relational-cultural therapy as a re-

14. Comstock et al., "Relational-Cultural Theory," 284.

15. Ibid., 74.

16. Ibid.

source starts with developing a healthy relationship between the therapist and African American women. A competent relational-cultural therapist can assist African American women in utilizing the therapeutic space and their relationship with the therapist to explore, create and build a setting in which dialogue and authenticity takes place. How well African American women can relate with the therapist is indicative of how well they can begin to build better growth fostering relationships with members in the society and with their family, church members and friends.

A major "bone of contention" for SAACW is their reception in the dominant culture, including the Black church. No matter how much traditional settings have changed in the contemporary culture, there are barriers to diversity. In fact, many of these settings are organized around marriage and family. Many complaints of SAACW are that the Black church is oblivious to the specific needs of its single population. In the *Narratives of the Church Environment*, Diane, Angie and Tracy challenge their rightful place as single women in a familial church environment. In engaging Diane, Angie and Tracy it becomes intrinsic for a relational-cultural therapist to acknowledge and attend to the issues of race, gender, culture, religion and God alongside understanding their beliefs, perceptions and emotions around singleness. As mentioned in this chapter and in previous chapters, African American women are inundated with many negative cultural images and perceptions. With the idyllic perceptions of family that are promoted in the dominant culture and pervasive stereotypes and images, some SAACW struggle to find their authentic place in both societal and religious contexts. Jana Marguerite Bennett, in *Water Is Thicker than Blood: An Augustinian Theology of Marriage and Singleness*, illustrates this point of singleness and how it takes on various meanings and interpretations.

> "Single" is, ironically, a complex word; it is often connotes separate individuals, as in "single combat." In households and living situations, it is used to describe various states of not being married; this description itself is inadequate, for "single" encompasses so many more complex situations than simple lack of marriage can describe. Those whose spouses have died are technically single, for example; so are people who have never married; small children are single, so are divorced parents, in the common way of thinking. More complex instances come to mind: are engaged people single? They are not quite married, but they are not quite single in the common use of the word . . . like many words, then "single" is not precise, or even an appropriately descriptive word on the whole; it is loosely applied

for many people. Many unmarried singles will say, "I don't know
how to be single well; clearly we humans are made to be married
instead." I think it is no mistake that just as we do not know how to
use the word "single" well and descriptively, so there is confusion
about how to live a good life as a "single person."[17]

Bennett names the "confusion" that follows the status of "singleness," yet a
culturally competent therapist explores some of the relational complexities
and diverse states of singleness that shape SAACW's identity development.
As a therapeutic resource for SAACW, relational-cultural therapy addresses
some of the critical sociocultural factors and taboo subjects that are prevalent in the African American community. For SAACW, the therapeutic
space supports them in "airing" their grievances and in examining other
life-changing events. Nancy Boyd Franklin, in *Black Families in Therapy*,
explains the challenges of single women from a multi-system lens and gives
insight on the therapeutic needs of this population. She posits that some
single women have pessimistic views about marriage and the possibilities
of ever marrying, there is an increase of educated and professional African
American women having children alone or adopting particularly those in
their late thirties and early forties, and there are African American wom-
en who have chosen to be in destructive relationships because there is a
shortage of African American men.[18] Boyd-Franklin sights the shortage as
endemic to high incarceration rates, under-education, under-employment
and drug usage.[19] She also expounds on the socialization of African American women and the significance of both positive and negative male-female
familial relationships that have been modeled by older females in their
family unit. Ultimately, these factors impact their relationships with African American men, for better and worse. Again, these are various cultural
factors that have a major impact SAACW. Narratives are a powerful tool in
working with single African American women as the therapist's capacity
to understand and connect with the stories of African American women
is crucial to their relational development. Narratives are a valuable tool
for exploring familial, communal and religious relational dynamics. How
SAACW relate with their stories and make meaning of their stories in the
context of people, systems and culture can be useful in relational-cultural
therapy to build better growth enhancing relationships.

17. Ibid., 84.
18. Ibid., 96.
19. Ibid., 86.

In working with SAACW, it is important to draw out their inner strengths and resources as competent and complete women rather than women who are lacking in some way. As noted in the discussion on connection and disconnection, many of these inner strengths and resources are gained from their upbringing, family/extended family, spirituality and other diverse resources.[20] This is also significant as African American women have painful histories of slavery and currently rely on their inner strengths and resources to challenge their reception in the society. Therefore, I believe that relational-cultural therapy is a collaborative approach that can assist SAACW in their understanding of the self from a position of health and strength rather than a position of pathology or deficiency. A distinctive relational-cultural therapy addresses the "real" life experiences of women.[21]

For SAACW, a healthiness of the self means accepting the "self" or "being oneself" amid so many pervasive myths, stereotypes, assumptions and beliefs. In general, society dictates that single people are "incomplete" because they are unmarried. Although some SAACW are open to marriage, it is not an all-consuming goal that directs their lives. A healthier understanding of singleness means not feeling stuck in societal and religious expectations—relationally, vocationally, culturally and sexually.

Because there are so many expectations and interpretations of singleness, a therapeutic space that honors their humanness, their feelings and beliefs is essential to their relational well-being. As a relational-cultural therapist is instrumental in creating a space where growth autonomy occurs, a therapist can explore with them their substantial place in the world. SAACW complain that there are societal judgments against them because of their choices and sexual preferences. Not feeling like they are alone or vile and that something is "wrong" with them for being single and sexual beings is significant in the therapeutic setting. They feel a deep sense of dissatisfaction because of how they are perceived or even shamed by those in their social and religious circles.

A relational-cultural therapist creates a liberating therapeutic space to help them feel accepting of their "whole" selves and their sexual freedom despite some of the rigidity that is evident in the dominant religious culture. In the Black church culture, SAACW are inflicted with certain polarities, they are either "whores" for embracing their sexuality or they are either castigated as "super saintly women" for upholding a holy life that is devoid

20. Ibid., 69.
21. Ibid., 64.

of sexual pleasure and that is pleasing to God. An astute therapist will have conversations about sexuality as a means of empowerment against the paradoxical lenses that are interpreted in the religious culture. We can learn more about the negative impact of African American women's sexuality as it relates to their relational development within themselves and within the social and religious milieu. Relational-cultural theory examines the concept of "power over" "whereby people can feel safe and productive by exercising power over others, keeping others in a less advantaged position."[22] The Black church uses its power to enforce the sexual identity of its female members. Kelly Brown Douglas, in *Sexuality and the Black Church*, states that the Black church has inherently borrowed many of the White cultural exploitation whereby Black women's appreciation for their embodied Black selves is sinful.[23] Therefore, a therapeutic counseling setting that invites African American women to formulate an empowered sense of agency and action as it pertains to their "bodies" is vital to their relational sexual health and well being.

Relational-cultural theory as a practical approach examines the "empowered" sense of self that permits "clarity about one's choices within a relationship and ones feelings and actions as a competent self."[24] A healthiness of the self lies in honoring their experiences as they make meaning and sense of the world. Relational-cultural therapy assists SAACW in revisiting their social, familial and religious relationships, but it also assists them in processing how they want to be in world and where they feel most comfortable and authentic as single women. "Authenticity is the ability to form relationships where one can state one's feelings to others," including personal values, beliefs, interest and experiences.[25]

In order for SAACW to reach a place of health, relational-cultural therapy acknowledges what is called "naming the unnamable" to facilitate growth enhancing relationships specifically for African American women.[26] Naming is "acknowledging and validating all their experiences, thereby influencing authentic, positive, and differentiated connections to the self, others, and society at large."[27] I return to the *Narratives of the Church*

22. JMBTI, "Power Over."
23. Ibid., 123.
24. Ibid., 71.
25. Ibid., 66.
26. Ibid., 77.
27. Ibid.

Environment in which the power of "naming" is cathartic for Diane, Angie and Tracy as they express their anger in being treated as "invisible," the "other" and the "outsider" in their places of worship. Hence, a healthiness of the self means embracing their honest emotions and reactions. Jean Baker Miller, in *Toward a New Psychology of Women*, states that "emotionality is a part and parcel of every human being . . . we have a long tradition of trying to dispense with, or least control or neutralize, emotionality, rather than valuing, embracing, and cultivating its contributing strengths."[28] Diane, Angie and Tracy claim their own sense of empowerment, emotionality and agency amid their struggles within the Black church.

As noted by Bennett, there is no monolithic expression and interpretation of singleness. Therefore, a healthiness of the self means living a "good" single life that is relative to expression for each woman. In their *Narratives of the Church Environment*, Diane eloquently states she doesn't need marriage to "cure" her singleness. Angie says she is single because she "chooses" to be single. Tracy articulates that people can't "pretend" that she doesn't exist. All of these statements illustrate their strengths and abilities in debunking the common stereotypes that exist for SAACW in the Black church. There are many SAACW who will never marry and some are accepting of this notion and some are not. For others it does not matter. So embracing a healthy relational existence with family, friends and church family is central to the growth fostering relationship that is important to this approach. It does not solve the negative reactions that they may receive from these relationships, but it invites them in developing a healthy existence within the confines of these sometimes conflicting relationships. It may even invite dialogue and conversation within the boundaries of these relationships. Family and extended family, community and spirituality play a significant role in the African American culture and therefore, African American women work toward building better relations within these polarities of family, church and singleness. The role of conflict is examined further.

> A relational-cultural approach recognizes that all relationships are punctuated by disconnections, misunderstandings and conflict. Connecting in real growthful way with others is not always harmonious or comfortable; we all experience fear, anger and shame. We move away to protect ourselves, particularly if we are not met with empathic responsiveness or if we feel we do not matter to the other person. But when we renegotiate these inevitable

28. Baker Miller, *Toward a New Psychology*, 38.

disconnections, the relationship is enhanced and personal feelings of well being, creativity, and clarity increase.[29]

A relational-cultural approach emphasizes power and agency in connection. There is the temptation of SAACW to retreat in isolation because of the pervasive assumptions about singleness; however, how well they negotiate and continue to renegotiate their authentic place is essential to healing and growth. SAACW can bring awareness to these conflicting assumptions so that those in power can not only listen and but be responsive to their needs. This takes place in what is called mutual empowerment and mutual empathy where both parties move with a sense of mutual respect, aliveness and clarity.[30] The relationship is built on "engagement" which means being present and caring about the relationship as well as the individual.[31] Jean Baker Miller explains the "five good things"[32] that transpire in growth fostering relationships:

1. *Zest or high energy*: the feeling of vitality, aliveness, and energy that results when a real sense of connection, togetherness with, and joining by the other person(s) is experienced.

2. *Action*: the ability to choose, to move, or to do "in the moment of the immediate exchange." Each participant in the dialogue has an important impact on the other that leads to action beyond the immediate interaction.

3. *Knowledge*: the enlarged and more accurate picture of self and the other that develops in relationship. Each participant learns more about her relationship with another/others and how it influences her own relational experience.

4. *Self-Worth*: this develops out of recognition, acknowledgment, and understanding of one's experience by those who are important to her.

5. *A greater sense of connection and a desire for more connection*: this involves the strong bond that develops between participants in the relationship and their desire for more connection based on interactions that have taken place until the present.

29. Ibid.
30. Ibid.
31. Ibid.
32. Jenkins, "Stone Center," 68.

IN CONCLUSION

The relational-cultural approach to counseling identifies obstacles to growth fostering relationships. For African American women there are matters such as race, gender, class that impact their relational development within the dominant culture. This chapter explores the relational development of SAACW through the lens of connection and disconnection within the Black church. Marriage is viewed as a healthy connection within the Black church while singleness is a distorted view of connection and disconnection. SAACW are perceived as relational "misfits" because they are unmarried. The goal in using a relational-cultural competency is to provide a resource for SAACW as they reach a place of acceptance and healthiness of the self from various multicultural contexts and understandings.

Chapter 8

"God Made Us Special in the Bonds of Sisterhood"

PASTORAL MINISTRY AND THE "MARY AND MARTHA ETHICS OF PASTORAL CARE" IN THE BLACK CHURCH

This chapter serves as a practical resource for the Black church as a means of connecting and engaging with the single adult population, namely SAACW in midlife. "Diane," "Angie" and "Tracy" named the difficulty in connecting with their churches as older midlife single women. Single adults are significant and valuable persons in the society as well as the Black church. Yet, they are misrepresented in these environments as they face many challenges daily. As the Black church is a place of worship, connection and support for SAACW, how can the Black church begin to assist them in their specific needs in the twenty-first century? SAACW face many challenges of race, gender, class and marital status along with transitioning into midlife and growing older. Facing the possibility that they may never marry or have biological children is a reality for SAACW. However, creating lives that are self-sustaining and self-fulfilling is important to their well-being. This chapter therefore, summarizes some common beliefs about SAACW and counters them as a means of providing practical ministry and support. The chapter also serves as a pastoral care resource for SAACW in what I call the "Mary and Martha Ethics of Pastoral Care."

PASTORAL MINISTRY FOR SAACW IN MIDLIFE

A common complaint that is voiced by SAACW is that the *Black church doesn't know what they need to feel included.* One of the ways in which the Black church can engage and connect with SAACW is in creating community with them. Their communities could be more intentional in including them in all aspects of the church and fellowship instead of SAACW having to search for these opportunities. Creating a common interest group with diverse people from all aspects life and diverse marital status could foster a community that is more inclusive for all persons, but more importantly inclusive to SAACW. This could present opportunities for the community to get to know one another inside and outside of the regular church setting.

In contrast to developing community and groups with persons from diverse backgrounds, there is the controversial issue of developing community and groups solely with SAACW. The participants in this study, Diane, Angie and Tracy had mixed reviews of a singles' midlife Christian women's group. Two of the participants (Angie and Tracy) did not have a problem with a singles' midlife Christian women's group with women of a similar demographic: midlife ages 40–55, childless, and never been married. The other participant (Diane) did have a problem with being singled out as a *single* Christian woman, but she was not opposed to developing a women's group that catered to other interests in her life. Creating a singles' midlife Christian women's group is dependent upon the needs of the women in the congregation. Let the women guide the development of a singles' midlife Christian women's group, if there is a need. Be very clear about the guidelines and objectives for this group with the understanding that some will not be a part because it makes them feel "singled out" from the communal life of the church. However, there are some who will participate and find a need for this type of support. Therefore, creating a singles' midlife Christian women's group that doesn't focus on marriage per se, but focuses on how to live purposeful, meaningful and holistic lives regardless if marriage is in the future or not, is in order. Moreover, a singles' midlife Christian women's group can also be resourceful for those who wish to participate as a means of sharing life experiences.

Another means of engaging SAACW so that they feel included in the Black church is in directly asking what their needs are so that they can discuss how they would like to be included in the life and activity of the Black church. This may include written surveys with the intention of coming together as a group to talk about their concerns and needs. I encourage direct conversation so that many of the assumptions, beliefs and myths can be dispelled. Moreover, a direct approach can enlighten church leadership about the complexities of SAACW in the twenty-first century.

A second complaint that is voiced by SAACW is that *they are often labeled as "incomplete," "abnormal," "diseased" "suspicious," not "whole" persons*. The term "complete" is often associated with those who are married. The assumption is that married couples are complete and normal, while single individuals are incomplete and abnormal. The Black church can create more inclusive conversations and awareness of all types of diversity, i.e., ethnicity, sexual orientation, religion, gender, class, socioeconomic class and marital status. Because marriage is a significant aspect of our society, it is considered the normal path for the single adult. There are assumptions about what is "complete" and "normal" that are attached to one's marital status. These assumptions directly impact persons who are unmarried, i.e., divorced, widowed, single parents, cohabiting and SAACW (single, never been married, no children). I recommend incorporating more inclusive language from the pulpit in sermons, litanies, prayers, hymns and teaching so that singleness is legitimated as a normal path and normal state for persons who are unmarried. Using less patriarchal language and more inclusive familial language helps to dispel such labels as *"incomplete," "abnormal," "diseased" "suspicious," and not "whole" persons*. All human beings, including those who are married, divorced, widowed, cohabiting, single with children, single without children and SAACW, are susceptible to frailties in life. All human beings experience aloneness, loneliness, sexual desires, anger, fear, conflict and shame. Normalizing these aspects helps to dismantle some of the myths and assumptions of singleness. All persons are whole persons and normal persons with human frailties. Church leadership training, theological training and ministry awareness can assist in "normalizing" SAACW as "whole" persons. Since all persons experience aloneness, loneliness, sexual desires, anger, fear, conflict, shame and other specific internal issues, there may be a need for SAACW to seek therapy for issues that are too difficult to manage. Counseling referrals are important to SAACW and a supportive church leadership can assist in these endeavors.

A third complaint and belief in the Black church is that *SAACW are not considered as a traditional family like their married counterparts*. Although the Black church has served as an extended family for the African American community, singleness is not considered "family" in the traditional sense of marriage and family. The Black church as an extended family does provide resources and care for SAACW, but it also mimics the society in terms of how it perceives marriage and family as a normative state for all persons. Utilizing SAACW in leadership increases their visibility, participation and "belongingness" in the Black church. For every sermon that uses a family illustration make sure that a single family illustration is also used as a point of reference to counterbalance the diversity of families in the twenty-first century.

A fourth complaint is that *SAACW are more readily available to serve in the Black church.* The assumption is that SAACW are older women who have expendable time and are always free to serve within the Black church. An appropriate pastoral response is the conviction that work is a shared responsibility for all persons, married, divorced, widowed and single, in the household of God. Church leadership cannot assume that SAACW are available for every task within the Black church because they are unmarried. Moreover, this assertion perpetuates many of the nurturing roles that African American women have inherited as they are considered the well-oiled machine and the "backbone" of the Black church. Singleness does not mean that SAACW are lonely or bored and are looking for "something" to do. Church leadership can be more sensitive to the interests of SAACW outside the parameters and functioning of the Black church.

A fifth complaint is that *SAACW need married couples and married church leadership to assist them in singleness.* The complaints of the research participants, Diane, Angie and Tracy, is that the church leadership who organize and structure "singles" events can't relate to them because they are married couples who have been married for a very long time. In short, they have no idea what it is like to be "40–50 years old and single in the twenty-first century." The church leadership and ministers who are married are not the authority on singleness because it's not something that they live daily. In certain instances SAACW like to be "ministered" to by people who are single like themselves, someone who can relate to the issues of singleness, persons who can "speak their language." In understanding the pastoral care needs of the older singles in the Black church, church leadership can support SAACW with workshops and conferences that are led by singles with similar demographics. Again, this is in keeping with hearing the needs and concerns of the single population in the Black church.

The last complaint is that *SAACW are sexually immoral women.* SAACW are not always consumed with having sex. The assumption is that African American women are "Jezebels" who are in search of a sexual outlet.

SAACW want to be treated as adults who are capable of making credible decisions about their sex, sexuality and spirituality. Sexuality and spirituality are challenging within many churches including the Black church. However, having discussions about sex, sexuality and spirituality as a healthy "blessing" from God and a healthy aspect of being human opens the door for rich dialogue and understanding. Being Christian does not mean separating oneself from their sexuality or spirituality. Sex does not make one "sinful." Inviting academicians and theologians to lead discussion groups on sex, sexuality and spirituality can help foster dialogue and challenge some of the negative perceptions of African American women and tackle the taboo subject of sex, sexuality and spirituality within the Black church.

"MARY AND MARTHA ETHICS OF PASTORAL CARE" FOR SAACW IN MIDLIFE

Over the past fifteen years of ordained ministry, I have facilitated women's ministry groups attempting to create a community of health and well-being for African American women. However, this process of health, well-being, nurture, care, transformation and empowerment is not one that evolves overnight. It is an evolving process that happens over a period of time and intentionality in examining the self. Therefore, the "Mary and Martha Ethics of Pastoral Care" is the intentional self-care that is rendered by SAACW in midlife. It is a model of care in which they learn to bless themselves as unmarried women. Self care has several tapestries that are spiritual, sexual, psychological, emotional, intellectual and physical. Learning to bless those "better parts" is essential to their well being and self-care.

Why is the biblical image of Mary and Martha an important model of pastoral care for SAACW? Mary and Martha are single women who challenged their roles within the society. Mary and Martha both worked individually and collectively as single women in a time period where traditional marriage and family was upheld. Mary and Martha represent a powerful image for SAACW as they claim their personhood, womanhood and self autonomy. On numerous occasions, I've crafted sermons using Luke 10:38–42 with Mary and Martha as a theological metaphor for individuals seeking balance, wholeness and self-care. God creates women and all human beings with complex emotions, feelings, attributes and talents. Mary and Martha as a group model of pastoral care invites SAACW to evaluate the different seasons, developments and stages in their lives as God has created them. There are seasons that God requires them to work and there are seasons that God requires them to reflect, rejoice, celebrate and rest. Mary and Martha reflect the different sides of SAACW that they must learn to integrate.

Because SAACW are often misrepresented in the Black church, a pastoral care group facilitates a space in which they may care for themselves. As has been reiterated throughout this research, there is no perfect image and role of singleness. Therefore, SAACW define their "better parts" and needs as they journey with other women. I return to the image of Mary and Martha as a model that supports the ethic of pastoral care and SAACW creating those supportive networks of women. The "Mary and Martha Ethics of Pastoral Care" is a group of women who assist and challenge each other in the journey of self-care. This network of friendships and relationships is comprised of SAACW who are from different walks of life and who support one another to become whole persons. The "Mary and Martha Ethics of Pastoral Care" serves as a support group to help foster dialogue, self-care and celebration through established networks of SAACW.

"MARY AND MARTHA ETHICS OF PASTORAL CARE" GROUP

For this research, I facilitated a women's group with the research participants Diane, Angie and Tracy to discuss how they would support one another in a group setting. Listed below are my observations and suggestions in facilitating a "Mary and Martha Ethics of Pastoral Care" group along with their responses to the group questionnaire.

A "Mary and Martha Ethics of Pastoral Care" group *shares experiences with the understanding that their experiences impact one another.* The group process allows them to share their vast experiences so that they not only learn from one another but can become more sensitive and supportive to each other's needs. Second, the group process *allows SAACW to "sound off" with one another* and *share the "heart"* of what's bothering them so that they can be heard, held and encouraged. Third, this group *shares personal narratives and stories in a safe space.* The group setting allows them to talk about what's going on with them without judgment and it involves listening and not always giving advice. Sometimes they don't need advice but they do need someone to listen and allow them to speak their truth. Fourth, this group *examines destructive societal stereotypes and myths.* SAACW are given a bad rap in the media and therefore this group provides challenge, support and dialogue in areas that impact their well-being and livelihood. Fifth, a "Mary and Martha Ethics of Pastoral Care" group *shares female bonds and mentoring for SAACW*. There are numerous SAACW that attend church regularly and they suffer in silence. Therefore, this group gives support for those women who are silenced by many internal and external factors that impact their mental, spiritual, physical and emotional well-being. Sixth, this group *learns to love, celebrate, laugh and live life to the fullest*. Celebration and enjoying specific interest is important in loving the self and in establishing healthy self-care. Finally, a "Mary and Martha Ethics of Pastoral Care" group *develops their own spiritual practices and self-care rituals and resources* that assist them in connecting with themselves and God.

Group Questionnaire

How Can Women Support Each Other in Singleness?

1. What does it mean for you to come together as single women?
2. What issues do you have as single women individually/collectively?
3. What woman has been instrumental in your life and has helped you along the way and what wisdom or insight did she pass down to you?
4. What can you learn from each other as African American women?
5. What is your legacy to other African American women and children?
6. How do you nurture and care for yourself?

What does it mean for you to come together as single women?

Diane, age 43: "God made us special in the bonds of sisterhood."

Angie, age 48: "You need to know that there are women who care about you."

Tracy, age 53: "You need support to address a real need."

What can you learn from each other as African American women?

> Diane, age 43: "We come from different walks of life, different perspectives, but there is a commonality that we all have—a stream that draws us together."

> Angie, age 48: "We broaden ourselves as we learn about each other."

> Tracy, age 53: "We sharpen each other, iron sharpens iron and we sharpen each other."

How do you nurture and care for yourself?

> Diane, age 43: "You have to love yourself first and then you are free to love your neighbor."

> Angie, age 48: "I've learned self care the hard way—I do everything until I hit a wall."

> Tracy, age 53: "I honor where I am, my truth."

PASTORAL THEOLOGICAL REFLECTION

In this discourse, there have been many questions and existential concerns about the plight of single African American women in the society and the Black church. Pastoral theology takes into account SAACW and their contextual realities and experiences. Because God and Jesus embody love, then that love manifests in the concerns and present realities of SAACW. Intrinsic to all human beings is the need for love and connection. Some SAACW desire a tangible extension of God's love through loving, committed and sometimes marital relationships. Similarly, there is the extension of God's love that is manifested in the nurture and care of the self. Pastoral theology critically reflects upon the faith questions that arise out of the ministry, care and concern of God's people. SAACW expressed their need for nurture, care and acceptance from the communities in which they serve. Because God and Jesus embody love then that love should be evident both within and without the Black church. The questions presented in the "Mary and Martha Ethics of Pastoral Care" group give insight into the practical ministry of self-care and support networks. Community for SAACW means "learning from one another," "formulating bonds of sisterhood," "love of self" and "a stream that draws them together."

In conclusion, a major emphasis in this research has been to bring awareness to singleness as it impacts SAACW in the twenty-first century. To date there has been much dialogue in the contemporary culture about the plight of single African American women. However, there has been limited dialogue and scholarly research into the pastoral theological concerns of SAACW in midlife. As I am an African American female pastoral theologian and a single African American Christian woman, it is my intent to give a different perspective of the midlife African American female population that resides in the Black church. Singleness is a normative way of being; however, the Black church's response to the multitude of single women that attend Black church denominations is very minimal. What has been espoused in this discourse is the number of single African American women that fill the pews of the Black church and therefore it begs to question the ministry that is in place to address the diverse needs and concerns of this growing population. This research emphasized the voices of SAACW in midlife as a means of exploring their emotional, psychological, spiritual, sexual and ethical lives. In the very present future, I am hopeful that singleness may be viewed as an acceptable and natural state that is embraced both in the Black church and contemporary culture.

Appendix 1

Research Participants Consent Form

TITLE OF STUDY:

Exploring the Psychosocial and Psycho–spiritual Dynamics of Singleness Among African American Christian Women in Midlife

PRINCIPAL INVESTIGATOR:

Christina Hicks
christina.hicks@emory.edu

PROJECT DESCRIPTION AND PURPOSE:

I am a doctoral student at Emory University enrolled in the Doctorate of Theology in Pastoral Counseling (ThD) program. You are asked to take part in this research study on singleness as it impacts Christian African American women in midlife, between the ages of 40 to 55. Approximately, 3 women will participate in an interview for this research study. The data will be used to give insight on the psychological and spiritual needs of single Christian African American women.

PROCEDURE:

The study will require a one hour commitment for the interview portion of the research and will take place in a designated room on Beulah Heights University campus or a designated church location according to your preference. You will be asked several questions on your beliefs, convictions, and satisfaction as a single Christian African American woman. With your permission, I will tape the interviews. Immediately, these taped conversations will be transcribed and then destroyed.

RISKS AND BENEFITS:

I do not anticipate any risks to you participating in this study other than those encountered in day to day life. There are no benefits to you personally other than this being an opportunity to tell your story about your experiences as a single Christian African American woman.

CONFIDENTIALITY:

Your responses to interview questions will be kept confidential. At no time will your actual identity be revealed. Your information will be kept in a secure locked cabinet and no one else will have access to it. I will not use your name or information that would identify you in any publications or presentations.

RIGHTS TO WITHDRAW FROM STUDY:

Your participation in this study is completely voluntary, and you may refuse to participate or withdraw from the study at any time. In the event you choose to withdraw from the study all information you provide (including tapes) will be destroyed and omitted from the final paper.

CONTACT PERSONS:

If you have any questions or concerns about this research, please contact me at christina.hicks@emory.edu or (678) 499–8099. You may also contact my department chair Dr. Emmanuel Lartey who is supervising this work at elartey@emory.edu or 404–727–6594.

Any questions, concerns, suggestions or, complaints that are not being addressed by the principal investigator or any research related harm, please contact the Emory University Institutional Review Board at (404) 712–0720 or toll free at 1–877–503–9797.

AGREEMENT:

The nature and purpose of this research have been sufficiently explained and I agree to participate in this study. I understand that I am free to withdraw at any time.

_____   _____

Research Participant   Date

_____   _____

Principal Investigator   Date

Appendix 2

Group Participants Consent Form

TITLE OF STUDY:

Exploring the Psychosocial and Psycho-spiritual Dynamics of Singleness Among African American Christian Women in Midlife

PRINCIPAL INVESTIGATOR:

Christina Hicks
christina.hicks@emory.edu

PROJECT DESCRIPTION AND PURPOSE:

I am a doctoral student at Emory University enrolled in the Doctorate of Theology in Pastoral Counseling (ThD) program. You are asked to take part in this research study on singleness as it impacts Christian African American women in midlife, between the ages of 40 to 55. Approximately, 3 women will participate in a group interview for this research study. The data will be used to give insight on the psychological and spiritual health of single Christian African American women in communal settings.

PROCEDURE:

The study will require a one hour commitment for the group interview portion of the research and will take place in a designated room on Beulah Heights University campus or a designated church location according to your preference. You will be asked several questions on your beliefs, convictions, and satisfaction as a single Christian African American woman and the role the church plays in this. With your permission, I will tape the interviews. Immediately, these taped conversations will be transcribed and then destroyed.

RISKS AND BENEFITS:

I do not anticipate any risks to you participating in this study other than those encountered in day to day life. There are no benefits to you personally other than this being an opportunity to tell your story about your experiences as a single Christian African American woman.

CONFIDENTIALITY:

Your responses to interview questions will be kept confidential. At no time will your actual identity be revealed. Your information will be kept in a secure locked cabinet and no one else will have access to it. I will not use your name or information that would identify you in any publications or presentations.

RIGHTS TO WITHDRAW FROM STUDY:

Your participation in this study is completely voluntary, and you may refuse to participate or withdraw from the study at any time. In the event you choose to withdraw from the study all information you provide (including tapes) will be destroyed and omitted from the final paper.

CONTACT PERSONS:

If you have any questions or concerns about this research, please contact me at christina.hicks@emory.edu or (678) 499–8099. You may also contact my department chair Dr. Emmanuel Lartey who is supervising this work at elartey@emory.edu or 404–727–6594.

Any questions, concerns, suggestions or, complaints that are not being addressed by the principal investigator or any research related harm, please contact the Emory University Institutional Review Board at (404) 712-0720 or toll free at 1-877-503-9797.

AGREEMENT:

The nature and purpose of this research have been sufficiently explained and I agree to participate in this study. I understand that I am free to withdraw at any time.

_____   _____
Research Participant   Date

_____   _____
Principal Investigator   Date

QUESTIONNAIRE #1

1. What comes to mind when you think about your life as a *single* African American woman?

2. How do you feel about being in your 40's or 50's?

3. What are some concerns, feelings or attitudes that you have as you grow older?

4. How do your family/siblings react to you being a single?

5. What is your role in your family of origin?

6. How do the roles that you played in your family of origin influence you today?

7. How do your friends/girlfriends/married friends react to your singleness?

8. What is your meaning of family as a single woman? Is there such a thing as the ideal family?

9. What beliefs, myths or values do you have about being single?

10. What beliefs, myths or values do you have as an African American woman?

11. What role does the society and culture play in how you understand yourself as a single woman and as an African American woman?

12. Describe your strengths?

13. Describe your weaknesses?

14. As you reflect on your life, what are some lessons you've learned?

15. As you reflect on your life, what makes you the woman you are today?

16. What meaning does work have for you, current and in the future?

QUESTIONNAIRE #2

1. What comes to mind when you hear the statement there is a "shortage of good African American men for African American women?"

2. What have your past dating relationships been like with African American men?

3. What are your feelings toward marriage? Do you want to be married why or why not?

4. What are you feelings toward singleness? Do you like being single? Why or why not?

5. On any given day, what emotions come up for you as a single woman?

6. What is taking place when these emotions come up for you, what are the triggers?

7. Do you regret not having children why or why not? Have you accepted the possibility that you will not have biological children?

8. Define the authentic life you have assigned for yourself as a single woman?

9. What are your sexual needs as a single woman?

10. What choices and decisions have you made in regards to having sex as a Christian woman?

11. Do you limit yourself to having sex outside of marriage because you are a Christian? Why or why not?

12. Are you having sex with anyone at this time? How does it feel to be in that sexual relationship?

13. Do you feel *free* to have sex outside of marriage because you are a Christian? Why or why not?

14. What myths and beliefs do you have about sex as told by your family and church?

15. Does God approve or disapprove to you having sex outside of marriage? Why or why not?

16. Are you dating anyone at this time?

17. Discuss the best time of your life over any time period? Discuss the worst time of your life over any time period?

18. How do other women support you in your singleness?

QUESTIONNAIRE #3

1. Describe the role of religion in your life. Spirituality or belief in God? Religious affiliation? Religious activities? Religion as a means of survival, empowerment, strength, oppression?

2. What are your spiritual or religious practices that sustain you?

3. What does it mean to be a spiritual being? What makes you a spiritual being?

4. How does the church or faith affiliation support you as a single woman?

5. What images or messages were given to you by the church about finding a husband?

6. What do God and the Bible have to say about your singleness?

7. What purpose does God have for you in your singleness? How is God a barrier or life-giving to your singleness?

8. What role does God play in your singleness?

9. How do you think the church should treat singles?

10. Do you think the church is responsible for your singleness? Why or why not?

11. Do you have any regrets as a single woman? Did one get away?

12. Describe any desperate moments that you've had as a single woman?

13. Why do you think you are single at this time?

GROUP QUESTIONNAIRE

1. How can women support each other in singleness?

2. What does it mean for you to come together as single women?

3. What issues do you have as single women individually/collectively?

4. What woman has been instrumental in your life and has helped you along the way? What wisdom or insight did she pass down to you?

5. What can you learn from each other as African American women?

6. What is your legacy to other African American women and children?

7. How do you nurture and care for yourself?

8. Are there any issues that you would like to discuss in regards to your singleness that were not discussed in your individual sessions?

Bibliography

Ali, Carroll A. Watkins. *Survival and Liberation: Pastoral Theology in African American Context.* St. Louis: Chalice, 1999.

Anderson, Carol M., and Susan Stewart. *Flying Solo: Single Women in Midlife.* New York: Norton, 1994.

Banks, Ralph Richard. *Is Marriage for White People? How the African American Marriage Decline Affects Everyone.* New York: Penguin, 2011.

Baker Miller, Jean. *Toward a New Psychology of Women.* 2nd ed. Boston: Beacon, 1986.

Baker Miller, Jean, and Janet Surray. "The Stone Center Papers." 1985.

Barrick, Audrey. "Study: Christian Divorce Rate Identical to National Average." *Christian Post*, April 4, 2008. http://www.christianpost.com/news/study-christian-divorce-rate-identical-to-national-average-31815.

Belgave, Faye Z., and Kevin W. Allison. *African American Psychology: From Africa to America.* Los Angeles: Sage, 2014.

Bellis, Alice Ogden. *Helpmates, Harlots, and Heroes: Women's Stories in the Hebrew Bible.* Louisville: Westminster John Knox, 2007.

Bennett, Jana Marguerite. *Water Is Thicker than Blood: An Augustinian Theology of Marriage and Singleness.* Oxford: Oxford University Press, 2008.

Berliner, Kathy, et al. "Single Adults and the Life Cyle." In *Individual, Family, and Social Perspectives: The Expanded Family Life Cycle*, edited by Monica McGoldrick et al., 149–62. Boston: Allyn & Bacon, 2011.

Borysenko, Joan. *A Woman's Book of Life: The Biology, Psychology, and Spirituality of the Feminine Life Cycle.* New York: Riverhood, 1996.

Boyd-Franklin, Nancy. *Black Families in Therapy: Understanding the African American Experience.* 2nd ed. New York: Guilford, 2003.

Brown, Laura S., and Maria P. P. Root, eds. *Diversity and Complexity in Feminist Therapy.* New York: Routledge, 2013.

Brown Douglas, Kelly. *Sexuality and the Black Church: A Womanist Perspective.* Maryknoll: Orbis, 1999.

Browning, Sandra Lee. "Sharing a Man: Insights from Research." *Journal of Comparative Family Studies* 3 (31) 339–46.

Cannon, Katie G. "Sexing Black Women: Liberation from the Prisonhouse of Anatomical Authority." In *Sexuality and the Sacred: Sources for Theological Reflection,* edited by Marvin M. Ellison and Kelly Brown Douglas, 78–94. 2nd ed. Louisville: Westminster John Knox, 2010.

Collins, Catherine Fisher. "Commentary on the Health and Social Status of African American Women." Introduction to *African American Women's Health and Social Issues,* 1–11. West Port, CT: Praeger, 2006.

Comstock, Dana L., et al. "Relational-Cultural Theory: A Framework for Bridging, Relational, Multicultural and Social Justice Competencies." *Journal of Counseling & Development* 86 (2008) 279–87.

Coontz, Stephanie. *Marriage, a History: How Love Conquered Marriage.* New York: Penguin, 2005.

Cooper, Deborrah. "Black Churches Keep African American Women Lonely and Single." *Angry Black Woman Watch* (blog). June 20, 2010. https://abww.wordpress.com/2010/06/20/from-deborrah-cooper-black-churches-keep-african-american-women-single-and-lonely.

Culbertson, Philip. *Caring for God's People.* Minneapolis: Fortress, 2000.

Cozad Neuger, Christie. *Counseling Women: A Narrative Pastoral Approach.* Minneapolis: Fortress, 2001.

Creswell, John W. *Qualitative Inquiry and Research Design: Choosing among Five Traditions.* Thousand Oaks, CA: Sage, 1998.

Daly, Lois K., ed. *Feminist Theological Ethics: A Reader.* Louisville: Westminster John Knox, 1994.

Davis, Joyce E. "Single Ladies." *Ebony,* October 2012, 136–39.

Davis, Linsey, and Hana Karar. "Single, Black, Female—and Plenty of Company." ABCNews.com, December 22, 2009. http://abcnews.go.com/Nightline/single-black-females/story?id=9395275.

Davis, Ruth E. "Discovering 'Creative Essences' in African American Women: The Construction of Meaning around Inner Resources." *Women's Studies International Forum* 21 (1998) 493–504.

Day, Keri. *Unfinished Business: Black Women, the Black Church, and the Struggle to Thrive in America.* Maryknoll: Orbis, 2012.

Dell, Mary Lynn. "Will My Time Ever Come? On Being Single." *In Her Own Time: Women and Developmental Issues in Pastoral Care,* edited by Jeanne Stevenson-Moessner, 311–31. Minneapolis: Fortress, 2000.

Desmond-Harris, Jenee. "Myth-Busting the Black Marriage Crisis." *Theroot.com,* August 18, 2011. http://www.theroot.com/myth-busting-the-black-marriage-crisis-1790865391.

Douglas, Brown Kelly. *Sexuality and the Black Church: A Womanist Perspective.* Maryknoll: Orbis, 1999.

Duenwald, Mary. "Some Friends, Indeed, Do More Harm than Good." *New York Times,* September 10, 2002.

Dyson, Marcia L. "Can You Love God and Sex?" *Essence,* February 1999, 100.

Effird, James M. "Fornication." In *The Harper Collins Bible Dictionary,* edited by Paul J. Achtemeier, 349. San Francisco: Harper Collins, 1985.

Ehrman, Bart D. *The New Testament: A Historical Introduction to the Early Christian Writings.* New York: Oxford University Press, 2000.

Ellie. "Why Educated, Single Black Women Struggle to Marry?" *RelationshipTricks.com*. June 24, 2015. http://www.relationshiptricks.com/why-educated-single-Black-woman-struggle-to-marry.

Ellison, Marvin M., and Kelly Brown Douglas. *Sexuality and the Sacred: Sources for Theological Reflection*. 2nd ed. Louisville: Westminster John Knox, 2010.

Essence. "What It Means to Be 'Equally Yoked.'" *Essence*, February 22, 2011. http://www.essence.com/2011/02/22/what-it-means-to-be-equally-yoked.

Few, April L., et al. "Sister-to-Sister Talk: Transcending Boundaries and Challenges in Qualitative Research with Black Women." *Family Relations* 52 (2003) 205–13.

Fry Brown, Teresa L. *God Don't Like Ugly: African American Women Handing On Spiritual Values*. Nashville: Abingdon, 2000.

Gates, Henry Louis, Jr., and Evelyn Brooks Higginbotham. *African American Lives*. Oxford: Oxford University Press, 2004.

Gerald, Corey. "Feminist Therapy." In *Theory and Practice of Counseling and Psychotherapy*, 361–94. Belmont, CA: Brooks-Cole / Cengage Learning, 2013.

Gilchrist, Eletra S. "Neither an 'Old Maid' nor a 'Miss Independent,' Deflating the Negative Perceptions of Single African American Women Professors." In *Experiences of Single African-American Women Professors: With This Ph.D., I Thee Wed*, 177–200. Lanham: Lexington, 2013.

Gilkes, Cheryl Townsend. *If It Wasn't for the Women*. Maryknoll: Orbis, 2001.

Gordon, Eleanor, and Gwyneth Nair. *Public Lives: Women, Family and Society in Victorian Britain*. New Haven: Yale University Press, 2003.

Harris, Stephen. *The New Testament: A Student's Introduction*. 4th ed. Boston: McGraw Hill Higher Education, 2002.

Harvey, Steve. *Act Like a Lady: Think Like a Man*. New York: HarperCollins, 2009.

Herlihy, Barbara, and Gerald Corey. "Feminist Therapy." In *Theory and Practice of Counseling and Psychotherapy*, edited by Gerald Corey, 360–94. Belmont: Brooks/Cole, 2009.

Hill, Shirley A. "Marriage among African American Women: A Gender Perspective." *Journal of Comparative Family Studies* 37 (2006) 421–40.

hooks, bell. *Sisters of the Yam: Black Women and Self Recovery*. Boston: South End, 1993.

Horsley, Richard A. *1 Corinthians*. Nashville: Abingdon, 1998.

Hunter, Rodney, et al. *Dictionary of Pastoral Care and Counseling*. Nashville: Abingdon, 1990.

Iyer, Nalini. "Heterosexual Privilege." In O'Brien, *Encyclopedia of Gender and Society*, 1:418–22.

Jackson, Leslie C. "The New Multiculturalism and Psychodynamic Theory: Psychodynamic Psychotherapy and African American Women." In Jackson and Green, *Psychotherapy with African American Women*, 1–14.

Jackson, Leslie C., and Beverly Greene, eds. *Psychotherapy with African American Women: Innovations in Psychodynamic Perspectives and Practice*. New York: Guilford, 2000.

James, Shawn. "Why Most Black Women Will Remain Single for the Rest of Their Lives." James's blog. November 26, 2012. http://shawnsjames.blogspot.com/2012/11/why-most-black-women-will-remain-single.html.

JMBTI. "Power Over." Jean Baker Miller Training Institute, Wellesley Centers for Women, Wellesley College. https://www.jbmti.org/Our-Work/glossary-relational-cultural-therapy#power over.

————. "Relational-Cultural Theory." Jean Baker Miller Training Institute, Wellesley Centers for Women, Wellesley College. https://www.jbmti.org/Our-Work/relational-cultural-theory.

Jenkins, Yvonne M. "The Stone Center Theoretical Approach Revisited: Applications for African American Women." In *Psychotherapy with African American Women: Innovations in Psychodynamic Perspectives and Practice*, edited by Leslie C. Jackson and Beverly Greene, 62–81. New York: Guilford, 2000.

Johnson, Amanda, ed. *Our Voices: Issues Facing Black Women in America.* Chicago: Moody, 2009.

Johnson, Eric. "Nightline Face Off: Why Can't a Successful Black Woman Find a Man?" ABCNews.com, April 21, 2010. http://abcnews.go.com/Nightline/FaceOff/nightline-black-women-single-marriage/story?id=10424979.

Jones, Joy. "State of Black Marriage. *Ebony*, March 2011, 72–73.

Lartey, Emmanuel Y. *Pastoral Theology in an Intercultural World.* Cleveland: Pilgrim, 2006.

Lincoln, C. Eric, and Lawrence H. Mamiya. "Black Women, Black Men and the Black Church: Where Have All the Men Gone?" In *The Black Church and the African American Experience*, 274–308. Durham: Duke University Press, 1990.

Madden, Myron C. "Intimacy and Distance." In Hunter, *Dictionary of Pastoral Care and Counseling*, 594–95.

Marshall, Joretta L. "Sexual Identity and Pastoral Concerns: Caring with Women Who Are Developing Lesbian Identities." In *Through the Eyes of Women: Insights for Pastoral Care*, edited by Jeanne Stevenson Moessner, 143–66. Minneapolis: Fortress, 1996.

McGoldrick, Monica, et al. *Individual, Family, and Social Perspectives: The Expanded Family Life Cycle.* 4th ed. Boston: Allyn & Bacon, 2011.

Membis, Liane. "Does the Black Church Keep Black Women Single?" CNN.com, August 10, 2010. http://www.cnn.com/2010/LIVING/08/10/black.church.women.single/index.html.

Miller-McLemore, Bonnie J., and Brita L. Gill-Austern, eds. *Feminist and Womanist Pastoral Theology.* Nashville: Abington, 1999.

Mitchem, Stephanie V. Preface to *Introducing Womanist Theology.* Maryknoll: Orbis, 2002.

Nelson, James B. *Embodiment: An Approach to Sexuality and Christian Theology.* Minneapolis: Augsburg, 1978.

O'Brien, Jodi, ed. *Encyclopedia of Gender and Society.* Thousand Oaks, CA: Sage, 2009.

O'Connor, Pat. "Women's Friendships in a Postmodern World." In *Placing Friendship and Context: Structural Analysis in the Social Sciences*, edited by Rebecca G. Adams and Graham Allan, 117–35. New York: Cambridge University Press, 1998.

Phipps, William E. "Masturbation." In Hunter, *Dictionary of Pastoral Care and Counseling*, 691–92.

Rodrigue, Edward, and Richard V. Reeves. "Single Black Female BA Seeks Educated Husband: Race, Assortative Mating and Inequality." Brookings Institution report. April 9, 2015. https://www.brookings.edu/research/single-black-female-ba-seeks-educated-husband-race-assortative-mating-and-inequality.

Sanders, Kimberly Wallace. *Skin Deep Spirit Strong: The Black Female Body in American Culture.* Ann Arbor: University of Michigan Press, 2002.

Sahgal, Neha, and Greg Smith. "A Religious Portrait of African-Americans." PEW Research Study. January 30, 2009. http://www.pewforum.org/2009/01/30/a-religious-portrait-of-African-Americans.

Schaberg, Jane. "Luke." In *Women's Bible Commentary*, edited by Carol A. Newsom and Sharon H. Ringe, 363–93. Louisville: Westminster John Knox, 1992.

Schüssler Fiorenza, Elisabeth. *But She Said: Feminist Practices of Biblical Interpretation.* Boston: Beacon, 1992.

Schwartzberg, Natalie, et al. *Single in a Married World: A Life Cycle Framework for Working with the Unmarried Adult.* New York: Norton, 1995.

Sharp, Carolyn J. *Wrestling with the Word: The Hebrew Scriptures and Christian Believer.* Louisville: Westminster John Knox, 2010.

Simpson, Roona. "Bachelors and Spinsters." In O'Brien, *Encyclopedia of Gender and Society*, 1:51–52.

Smith, Wallace Charles. *The Church in the Life of the Black Family.* Valley Forge, PA: Judson, 1985.

Snorton, Teresa E. "What About All Those Angry Black Women?" In *Woman Out of Order: Risking Change and Creating Care in a Multicultural World*, edited by Jeanne Stevenson-Moessner and Teresa Snorton, 207–17. Minneapolis: Fortress, 2010.

Stack, Carol. *All of Our Kin: Strategies of Survival in a Black Community.* New York: Basic, 1974.

Staples, Robert. "Black Singles in America." In *Single Life: Unmarried Adults in Social Context*, edited by Peter J. Stein, 40. New York: St. Martin's, 1981.

Stein, Peter J., ed. *Single Life: Unmarried Adults in Social Context.* New York: St. Martin's, 1981.

Stevenson-Moessner, Jeanne, ed. *Women and Developmental Issues in Pastoral Care: In Her Own Time.* Minneapolis: Augsburg Fortress, 2000.

Stevenson-Moessner, Jeanne, and Teresa Snorton, eds. *Women Out of Order: Risking Change and Creating Care in a Multicultural World.* Minneapolis: Fortress, 2010.

Tavassoly, Iman. "Virginity." In O'Brien, *Encyclopedia of Gender and Society*, 2:874.

Thompson, Lisa B. *Beyond the Black Lady: Sexuality and the New African American Middle Class.* Urbana: University of Illinois Press, 2009.

Townes, Emilie M. *Breaking the Fine Rain of Death: African American Health Issues and a Womanist Ethic of Care.* New York: Continuum, 1998.

———. *Embracing the Spirit: Womanist Perspectives on Hope, Salvation & Transformation.* Maryknoll: Orbis, 1997.

———. *In a Blaze of Glory: Womanist Spirituality as Social Witness.* Nashville: Abingdon, 1995.

———, ed. *A Troubling in My Soul: Womanist Perspectives on Evil & Suffering.* Maryknoll: Orbis, 2002.

Trimberger, E. Kay. *The New Single Woman.* Boston: Beacon, 2005.

Wagner, Richard A. "Fictive Kinship." In *Marriage and Family Encyclopedia* (online), 1995. http://family.jrank.org/pages/630/Fictive-Kinship.html.

Walker, Alice. "Womanist." In *In Search of Our Mothers' Gardens: Womanist Prose*, xi–xii. San Diego: Harcourt Brace Jovanovich, 1983.

Walsh, Froma. "The New Normal Diversity and Complexity in 21st Century Families." In *Normal Family Processes, Growing Diversity and Complexity*, 3–27. New York: Guilford, 2012.

Ward, Jane. "Lesbian Stereotypes: Bull Dyke." In *Encyclopedia of Gender and Society*, edited by Jodi O'Brien, 1:491–93. Thousand Oaks, CA: Sage, 2009.

Whitener, Connie. "The Real Reasons Why So Many Black Women Are Single." http://www.examiner.com/article/the-real-why-so-many-Black-women-are-single.

Bibliography

Williams, Delores S. *Sisters in the Wilderness: The Challenge of God-Talk*. Maryknoll: Orbis,1993.

Wimberly, Edward P. *Recalling Our Stories: Spiritual Renewal for Religious Caregivers*. San Francisco: Jossey-Bass, 1997.